Vico's Axioms

Vico's Axioms The Geometry of the Human World

James Robert Goetsch, Jr.

Yale University Press New Haven and London

Designed by Sonia Scanlon. Set in Bodoni type by The Composing Room of
Michigan, Inc., Grand Rapids, Michigan. Printed in the United States of
America by BookCrafters, Inc., Chelsea, Michigan.

Library of Congress Cataloging-in-Publication Data

Goetsch, James Robert, 1956–
    Vico's axioms : the geometry of the human world / James Robert Goetsch.
        p.   cm.
    Includes bibliographical references and index.
    ISBN 0-300-06272-9
    1. Vico, Giambattista, 1668–1744. Principi di una scienza nuova.
2. Philosophy.   3. Rhetoric—Philosophy.   I. Title.
B3581.P74G64   1995
195—dc20   95-7649
                CIP

A catalogue record for this book is available from the British Library.

The paper in this book meets the guidelines for permanence and durability of
the Committee on Production Guidelines for Book Longevity of the Council on
Library Resources.

10 9 8 7 6 5 4 3 2 1

To Bev, Elizabeth, James, Sarah,
John Paul, and Rachael

Great straightness seems crooked,
Great skill seems clumsy,
Great eloquence seems awkward.

—Lao Tzu

An unapparent connection is stronger than an apparent one.

—Heraclitus

Contents

Abbreviations

A   *The Autobiography of Giambattista Vico*

AR   *The Academies and the Relation between Philosophy and Eloquence*

AW   *On the Most Ancient Wisdom of the Italians*

IO   *Institutiones oratoriae*

R   *Disputation with the Giornale de' letterati d'Italia*

Rh   Aristotle, *Ars rhetorica*

SM   *On the Study Methods of Our Time*

Preface

Vico's friends often seem less kind than his enemies. Not content with simply rejecting his claims, they praise the originality of his insights while denying the lucidity of his thought. And what is most often discounted is the coherence of his new science. So Alasdair MacIntyre writes that Vico's scattered insights are useful only when "detached from their place in the sterile systematics of Vico's new science." Vico's achievements, he adds, "have had to be rescued from Vico's system."[1] And Isaiah Berlin, who has done so much to revive contemporary interest in Vico, could nonetheless write of him that "all his philosophical works, and the *Scienza nuova* in particular, are an amalgam of sense and nonsense, an ill-assorted mass of ideas, some lucid and arresting, others shapeless and obscure, all jostling each other in the chaos of his astonishingly fertile, but badly ordered and overburdened mind."[2] Is Vico's thought no more than this?

The chief complaint of Vico's critics focuses on how he orders (or fails to order) his thought. His systematics are fruitless, his philosophical works the ill-assorted products of a badly ordered mind. Both Berlin and MacIntyre seem to agree with Descartes that "those who have the strongest power of reasoning, and who most skillfully arrange their thoughts in order to render them clear and intelligible, have the best power of persuasion, even if they speak only low Breton and have never studied rhetoric."[3] Does Vico, the Royal Professor of Latin Eloquence at the University of Naples—a student and teacher of rhetoric—fail to persuade us because his powers of reasoning are weak and his thoughts unclear? Perhaps.

But perhaps the order found in Vico's thought is one that is unfamiliar to us. As Vico notes in axiom II of his *Scienza nuova*, "It is [a] property of the human mind that whenever men can form no idea of distant and unknown things, they judge them by what is familiar and at hand" (122).[4] According to Vico, this is a *boria*, a conceit, that has caused error to arise whenever scholars have turned to consider the principles of humanity, for they then make their judgments "on the basis of their own enlightened, cultivated, and magnificent times" (123). In other words, as the old saying has it, some books are like mirrors: if an ape looks in, no saint will look back. For as Heraclitus notes, "Eyes and ears are evil witnesses for men who have barbarian souls" (fr. D 107).[5] Maybe Vico seems incoherent because we are.

I wish to try to read Vico on his own terms; to try to see if an unfamiliar sense of order and coherence can be found in Vico's new science.[6] In order to do so, I shall focus on the axiomatics of the *Scienza nuova* in the broader context of Vico's thought as a whole. An axiom, as a basic governing principle, or *archē*, of scientific knowledge, provides a key to the articulation of the principles of coherence peculiar to the system it operates within. So my central focus will be the order and coherence of Vico's new science, understood through an examination of its axioms. I argue that Vico's axioms fundamentally reject the deductive orientation of the new sciences that developed out of the Renaissance revival of mathematics and that culminated in the geometric method of rationalism (as exemplified in Descartes). Vico instead roots his science in the human world, finding his inspiration in a *philosophical* recovery of ancient rhetoric that is yet cognizant of the modern age. Vico's new science, then, transforms our understanding of human knowledge and transforms as well the meaning of such terms as *axiom*, *system*, *truth*, and *certainty*. In this new vision of human knowing, the accepted canons of epistemology are inverted, and it is the partisans of the mathematical paradigm whose essential lucidity comes into question. The term *science* thus becomes indeterminate, and we must decide anew the criteria of persuasion.

The genre of this work might be called history of philosophy, if by that we denote an attempt at an imaginative reconstruction of meaning, as opposed to a collection of facts: an attempt to identify with the making of meaning. Owen Barfield notes of the modern interpreter of Greek philosophy that "such a one can read Plato and Aristotle through from end to end, he can even write books expounding their philosophy, all without understanding a single sentence. Unless he has enough imagination, and even enough power of detachment from the established meanings or thought forms of his own civilization, to enable him to grasp the meanings of the fundamental terms—unless, in fact, he has the power not only of thinking, but of *unthinking*—he will simply re-interpret everything they say in terms of subsequent thought."[7]

I hold that the history of philosophy is the art of what Barfield called unthinking the obvious.[8] As Heraclitus notes, "An unapparent connection is stronger than an apparent one" (fr. 54). In this book I wish to unthink the apparent in Vico, using as my guide the unapparent treatment of Vico's thought found in the work of Donald Phillip Verene. Verene's work has become for me in this regard a sort of echo chamber of the unfamiliar, which I now wish to explore through the medium of a scholarly study "complicitous with institutional arrangements."[9]

In the first four chapters I describe the "system" of thought in which Vico's axioms operate, for it is impossible to understand how ordering principles operate without a sense of their context. These chapters serve as a general introduction to the thought of Giambattista Vico, with an eye toward explaining his axiomatics. In my presentation of Vico I am indebted to the work of Ernesto Grassi in *Rhetoric as Philosophy* and Owen Barfield in *Poetic Diction:* these thinkers have been instrumental in forming my understanding of both Vico and the crucial role of the imagination in any genuinely philosophical understanding.

These chapters concern Vico's *anabasis* (or heroic journey): his discovery of a new mode of knowledge through a descent from Renaissance humanism to the origins of human thought—with a corresponding ascent, holding a new science of human wisdom in his hands. In Chapter 5 I examine how the humanistic tradition embraced the bounds of time and place in the notion of the topos, or commonplace. Understanding becomes intimately involved with memory, a notion developed in the Renaissance under the rubrics of the theater of memory and the theater of the world. These concepts will prove essential in understanding Vico's intent in organizing the *New Science* as he does. In Chapter 6 I explore Vico's recovery of ancient rhetoric through a discussion of Aristotle's conception of rhetorical demonstration and enthymeme. An understanding of this rhetorical idea of order provides a basis for understanding the sense of order found in Vico's new science. Chapters 8 and 9 focus on the functioning of Vico's axioms in his new method of thought: how a grasp of the particular and the universal in history combine in the axioms, providing the commonplaces necessary to comprehend the human world.

Finally, as a work rooted in the art of topics, Vico's *New Science* is a book concerned not just with theory but with how human beings are to live amid the uncertainties of the human world. Vico's axioms circulate through his book of wisdom like blood in the body of knowledge. Like the rhetorical ordering principles they recall, the axioms seek to combine *logos* and *pathos*, reason and feeling, in a heroic attempt to understand the human condition eloquently, as a whole. But given the fact that Vico's science is found in an age of barbaric reflection, a Vichian axiomatics is at best a guide for an attempt at balance that will never quite succeed. Vico's axioms ultimately structure a geometry of melancholy.

This book results from a dialogue with many friends. I would particularly like to mention Donald Phillip Verene, Carl Page, Ann Hartle, Donald Livingston, Giuseppe Mazzotta, Nancy du Bois, and Molly Black Verene. The seeds of parts of the book first appeared as "Vico's Speculative Geometry" in the *Journal of Speculative Philosophy* 4 (1995). My thanks to the Pennsylvannia State University Press for permission to draw on that work. And finally, thanks to my wife, Beverly: dos pou stō kai tēn gēn kinēsō.

Vico's Axioms

1 Vico's Anabasis

Literally, the Greek word *katabainō* means "to dismount from a horse or chariot" or "to descend from the highlands to the coastal plain," and it has come to mean simply "to go or come down"—"to descend." A *katabasis*, then, generally was "a descent" or "a way down (especially to the nether world)." In a more metaphorical usage, it has also come to mean "the attainment of an end or purpose."[1]

The complementary term, *anabainō*, means literally "to mount a horse or chariot" or "to ascend from the coastal plains to the highlands," and thus, generally, "to go or come up" or "to ascend." An *anabasis*, therefore, was usually "an ascent" or "a way up." Metaphorically, it could also mean "to go back" or "to return to the beginning."[2] Thus one might say that in one sense a katabasis and an anabasis could coincide, for to go down in the sense of attaining one's end or purpose (katabainō) might also mean to go back in the sense of returning to the beginning (anabainō).

Understood in this way, a katabasis could be one and the same as an anabasis, making the art of attaining an end or purpose identical with the art of returning to an origin. This thought is compatible with the basic Vichian principle expressed in the *Scienza nuova* as general axiom CVI: "Doctrines must take their beginning from that of the matters of which they treat" (314).

As Max Fisch notes, this axiom, as the "controlling methodological postulate of Vico's new science . . . assumes that genesis, or becoming, is of the essence of that which the new science treats: that, at least for the new science, nascence and nature are the same."[3] Vico states in axiom XIV that "the nature of things [*natura di cose*] is nothing but their coming into being [*nascimento di esse*] at certain times and in certain guises" (147). In the following axiom, XV, he adds that "the inseparable properties of things [*cose*] must be due to the modifications or guise with which they are born. By these properties we may therefore verify that the nature or birth [*natura o nascimento*] was thus and not otherwise" (148).[4]

1

Vico's science is a science of *origins*. As such, its basic operative principle is that of a return to the *archē*, the basic governing root of the matter under investigation. The birth or origin of the subject of investigation is thus central: one must descend, as it were, to the origins, in order to make sense of any aspect of human making.

In his discussion of method in section IV of the *Scienza nuova*, Vico notes again that the path his science should follow is to "begin where its subject matter began." He states that "we must therefore go back" with the philologians and philosophers to fetch what interests us from the myths of the first humans: "Our treatment of it must take its start from the time these creatures began to think humanly." He also remarks upon the incredible difficulty of discovering the way the first human thinking arose, noting that we had "to descend from these human and refined natures of ours to those quite wild and savage natures, which we cannot at all imagine and can comprehend only with great effort" (338).

When faced with any "civil thing," our first question should always be, What are its *archai*, or governing roots? It is such reasoning as this, which thinks from the origins, that Vico calls logical proofs (345). Such proof operates in a way quite different from that of a deductive system, for it functions in terms of memory, and the logic of memory is not found in a linear series of linked truths.

Vico states that "in reasoning of the origins of things divine and human in the gentile world, we reach those first beginnings beyond which it is vain curiosity to demand others earlier; and this is the defining character of principles. We explain the particular ways in which they came into being; that is to say, their nature, the explanation of which is the distinguishing mark of science" (346). Such thinking operates in terms of a truly archaic logic—the logic of the descent.

Vico urges a heroic journey on us, an anabasis, which begins with a descent to the origins of humanity, which is at the same time an ascent in that it is a return to the beginning principles which structure the birth, growth, and end of human society. Vico's journey is thus a descent that is also an ascent, reversing the principles of coherence that are familiar to us. As Heraclitus notes, "The way up and down is one and the same" (fr. 60). This is also true for Vico of his method or way of inquiry. Euclid's elements present us with one model of a method; a way of approach to things that, as transformed in the Cartesian paradigm, presents us with a peculiar geometrical model for life and thought. Vico's elements offer us a different sort of model and a different way of inquiry. In the modern way of inquiry, as exemplified in Cartesianism, we only ascend—and we never look back. We ascend from particularity to universality, leaving behind the binding contingencies of humanity, the strictures of time and place, in our search for the exact functional technique that will allow us to adjust reality to our specifications.

Vico's anabasis is different: it is a return to the beginning, which is always firmly rooted in a time and a place, as a real birth must be. The *Scienza nuova* seeks to teach us how to undertake such an anabasis for ourselves; Vico becomes our guide on a journey to the netherworld, where we discover the roots of the great tree of human making and knowing. He becomes for us what the Italians call a *cicerone:* a guide who can show us the sights in a knowledgeable way and speak of them with eloquence.

When we ascend back to our place in our time, which Vico calls the third age, we must recollect these governing roots in order to make a new place for ourselves. In doing so we are able to discern both the pattern of our times and our place in it. We then become like the divine—though not identical with it. We achieve self-knowledge. Looking back on our path of inquiry each of us can say with Heraclitus, "I sought for myself" (fr. 101).

The self-knowledge to which Vico is directing us implies a sense of order and coherence alien to the bare categorical unity that has become the paradigm of knowledge (and self-knowledge) in our time. An investigation of how Vico's axioms circulate in the achievement of that self-knowledge is thus revelatory of a different kind of wholeness, which is based on eloquence and which always operates out of a sense of the whole.

The modern sense of the whole is based on what Vico calls *coscienza*, a kind of knowing in which we merely witness or observe one thing after another, and as a result coscienza has only certitude; it is flat and one-dimensional. The self reflects the kind of whole to which it is directed and itself becomes similarly flat and empty, a bare list of formal categories.

The Vichian sense of wholeness is based on another kind of knowing, *scienza*, or maker's knowledge. The self that reflects such a whole in the microcosmic-macrocosmic mirroring of self and world is three-dimensional, for it is based on truth rather than certainty, and finds in its knowledge a true wholeness. For as Vico notes in glossing Seneca, "This world is a paltry thing unless all the world may find [therein] what it seeks" (1096).

The Bare Ruined Choirs of the Renaissance

Vico's descent, as chronicled in his *Autobiography*, was not at first a conscious one (although he came to see it as providential). It began with an increasing dissatisfaction with the critical philosophy he found growing around him in Naples. This dissatisfaction drove him to adopt certain principles of Renaissance thought that were then falling into disrepute and decline. For Vico's descent began in the *Dämmerung*, the twilight, of the Renaissance.[5]

In the *Autobiography* Vico describes how he spent nine years in self-imposed exile as a tutor to the family of Don Domenico Rocca, studying the classics of the ancient world and the Renaissance, as well as the Latin language.[6] He notes that he then, with his newly won knowledge in hand, "returned to Naples a stranger in his own land, and found the physics of Descartes at the height of its renown among the established men of letters." Upon his return he discovered that the great achievements of Renaissance thought and literature, which had "contributed so much to poetry, history and eloquence that all Greece in the time of its utmost learning and grace of speech seemed to have risen again in Italy," were "now thought worthy only of being shut up in the cloisters" (*A* 132/16). Physics, metaphysics, medicine, law, and eloquent speech were all being eclipsed by the geometrical method of Descartes.

How can we characterize the main principles of Renaissance thought Vico saw as being eclipsed? What elements of the Renaissance can we point to that will help us make sense of Vico's response to the Cartesianism that surrounded him? These elements were, on Vico's account, placed into his life by providence. Vico's roots in the Renaissance are then more of "the causes, natural and moral, and the occasions of fortune . . . which were destined later to bear fruit in those reflections on which he built his final work, the *New Science*, which was to demonstrate that his intellectual life was bound to have been such as it was and not otherwise" (*A* 182/44). But before beginning my own account of these causes, it is necessary to say something about my method. My procedure here is *not* to trace Vico's intellectual development in terms of the actual sources he may have read (although I shall do this when it seems relevant). I am not attempting an intellectual biography in the standard sense, which would track down every reference to books Vico had or had not read and which would note the precise intellectual parentage of this or that distinct concept or thought.[7] Such studies are interesting and useful, but I wish to attempt what Vico did in his *Autobiography*: to give the causes of his development according to a perceived design of the whole.

I shall not claim that Vico read Nicholas of Cusa, for example, who I am about to cite, and that because of his reading, Nicholas of Cusa had this or that influence on Vico; but I do claim that an understanding of Nicholas of Cusa can help us understand the pattern of Vico's development (or descent) that I wish to narrate. Immediately after Nicholas of Cusa I cite Marsilio Ficino, whom we know Vico read. That Vico actually read Ficino is not significant; rather, an understanding of some aspect of Ficino facilitates our gaining a certain perspective on Vico's descent, which allows us a certain view of the whole.

In proceeding in this way I am following the intent of Vico's comment on the nature of the fable: "So that, if we consider the matter well, poetic truth is metaphysical truth, and physical truth which is not in conformity with it should be considered false. Thence springs this important consideration in poetic theory: the true war chief, for example, is the Godfrey that Torquato Tasso imagines; and all the chiefs who do not conform throughout to Godfrey are not true chiefs of war" (205).

As Donald Phillip Verene notes, the *New Science* itself is a sort of metaphysical fable, which creates a true narration of the recollective imagination. Such truth, for Vico, gives access to "the facts" but does not arise from an inductive consideration of them. Instead, this truth "is generated as images that actually contain the providential nature of reality."[8] I intend in my account to imitate in some small way the Vichian method: to concern myself with the philosophical truth of Vico's ideas rather than to examine the "plain" historical data. The historical data are useful, but only as *points* to help generate the *perspective* of the whole.

My procedure is therefore different from that of Michael Mooney, who in *Vico in the Tradition of Rhetoric* also gives an account of Vico's relation to humanist culture. Mooney proceeds precisely by attempting to link Vico's fundamental insights into a one-to-one correspondence with various insights of the rhetorical tradition. His thesis, then, amounts simply to the view that Vico was, as it were, the most comprehensive—and partisan—synthesizer of the Ciceronian tradition that we have.

Mooney states that the fact that "Vico was a humanist—in the most traditional sense—is incontestable."[9] As a humanist, Vico's task was, in the manner of Cicero, "to gather up the fragments of learning and bring them to life through speech—this ancient Ciceronian ideal Vico took for his professional task."[10] In light of this, Mooney views Vico's claim to have achieved an actual metaphysics of history as exaggerated.[11] Vico's science is new for Mooney only in that it anticipates a comprehensive approach to the problems of culture and society that found fruition in the social sciences of our own century, in the works of men life "Tönnies, Durkheim, and Weber, and to their manifold followers in our own bright times."[12]

Mooney finds himself ultimately at one with Isaiah Berlin and Alasdair MacIntyre. Each apparently believes that Vico, however much a genius, never quite got it *right* (that is, clear and certain): "Had he had more time," Mooney tells us, "he might have expressed himself on these matters, as on many matters, with greater clarity and thoroughness than he in fact achieved."[13]

The problem with this is that Mooney's analysis literalizes Vico's relation to the Renaissance, when instead we must look for a more subtle connection. Vico was not simply trying to be a new Cicero. The great Roman orator was not melancholy enough to be a metaphysical rhetorician. Karl-Otto Apel states that "Vico is a humanist truly the conclusive end, the Owl of Minerva, of the Italian Renaissance Culture."[14] Here Vico is viewed as the completion of the Renaissance, as the one who ends it in the sense of giving it a meaning. Vico thus represents (to use the Hegelian idiom) an *Aufhebung* of Renaissance thought.

Viewed in this light, Vico is that thinker who, as Ernesto Grassi notes, "saw most deeply and fully the tradition of Italian Humanism in all its implications."[15] Grassi's statement reminds us that the elements of the Renaissance in which Vico was rooted were those of Italian humanism. I am not attempting to refer to the Renaissance as a whole—it is too large and complex a period for that. I am speaking specifically of Vico's appropriation and development of those strands of Renaissance thought that took rhetoric seriously; the work of the thinkers known as the *litterae* and those close to them, who devoted themselves to the study of letters. But that does not make Vico a nostalgic humanist. According to Nancy Struever, we "must recognize that Vico was reading for the *New Science* precisely the same texts that he used in [teaching] school, and was coming up with extremely different mediations."[16]

Vico is the "complete humanist" only in the sense that he understands the tradition better than it understands itself. He recognizes its limitations as well as its strengths. We must see that Vico's relation to the Renaissance is complicated and that although Vico began in the tradition of Renaissance humanism and rhetoric, he did not remain there. He descended *through* it to achieve something quite different.[17] As Verene notes, "Vico should be approached as an unfamiliar other, whose thought teaches doctrines much less close to us than we may wish to think."[18] If one does not understand this caution, one might find oneself in the ironic position of writing a whole work on Vico and nowhere in it demonstrating a grasp of one of his most fundamental general axioms, that "whenever men can form no idea of distant and unknown things, they judge them by what is familiar and at hand" (122).[19]

The Bond and Knot of the Universe

The first element of Renaissance thought that seems necessary for an understanding of Vico's descent is the idea of the microcosm—the metaphysics of self-knowing. Nicholas of Cusa, whose thought is itself a microcosm of much of the Renaissance, expresses it this way: "Now, human nature is that nature which, though created a little lower than the angels, is elevated above all the other works of God; it enfolds intellectual and sensible nature and encloses all things within itself, so that the ancients were right in calling it a *mikrokosmos*, or a small world."[20]

Before Nicholas of Cusa, in medieval times (and even stretching back to Plato's *Timaeus*), a traditional trope held that the human being was a miniature world, containing within itself all the elements of the universe and thus subject to all its forces.[21] Paracelsus expressed this view when he wrote:

> Since man is a child of the cosmos, and is himself the microcosm, he must be begotten each time anew, by his mother. And just as he was created of the four elements of the world even in the beginning, so he will be created in the future again and again. For the creator created the world once, and then he rested. Thus he also made heaven and earth and formed them into a matrix, in which man is conceived, born, and nourished as though in an outer mother. . . . Thus life in the world is like life in the matrix . . . for the matrix is the Little World and has in it all the kinds of heaven and earth.[22]

For Paracelsus, the human being "carries the stars within himself. . . . He is the microcosm, and thus carries in him the whole firmament with all its influences."[23] The human being, as a Little World, is the image of the surrounding world.

In medieval thought, redemption would mean redemption from the body and liberation from those influences.[24] But for Nicholas of Cusa, human beings were microcosms in a different sense. Finding themselves at the center of creation, where time and eternity intersect, humans unite in one being "the lowest level of intellectual reality and the highest reach of sensible nature and [are] thus a bond which holds creation together."[25] Human redemption would thus include the redemption of all creation as well, which implies that the physical universe is to be transformed through the agency of humankind.

Nicholas of Cusa rejected the tendency to locate meaning solely in another world and posited a concrete living subject as the focal point of creation and creaturely activity.[26] He thus emphasized the role of humans as temporal and historical beings. Ernst Cassirer states that for Nicholas of Cusa, "man is completely enclosed in time; indeed, he is completely entrapped in the particularity of any given moment and completely enmeshed in the conditions of that moment; and yet, despite all this, man proves to be a *deus occasionatus*. He remains enclosed within his own being, never transgressing the limits of his own specifically human nature. But inasmuch as he develops and expresses every facet of his nature, man represents the divine in the form and within the limits of the human."[27] As microcosm, humanity is viewed as integral to the world in which it exists, and the essence of this integration is the force of the human mind in free creation.[28] In order to be fully human, the human being must freely transform the world. Here we find combined with the notion of the microcosm the idea of the human as the being who creates in imitation of God.

The Human Creator

For the Renaissance thinker, God had made humankind in his own image, and thus godlike. And humankind was nowhere more godlike than in its creative activity. As Cassirer notes, for Nicholas of Cusa, "the mind attains genuine insight not when it reproduces external existence, but only when it 'explicates' itself and its own nature."[29]

This process was epitomized for Nicholas of Cusa in mathematics, which finds its reality as an expression of human making. In such making the human mind creates for itself its own mental world: "Just as God is active *ad extra*, creating real things and natural forms, so also man can bring forth rational things and artificial forms. . . . The mathematical sciences have their origin in man's mind, just as real beings have theirs in the divine intellect."[30] In acting in this way, as a maker of his or her own world, the human being becomes so much an express image of God that he or she might be said to be a kind of divinity—a "created god."[31]

Marsilio Ficino took up the idea of the microcosmic created god in a way that affirmed not only mathematical making and intellectual activity but artistic production as well. Ficino was interested in "the miracle of beauty . . . the miracle of artistic form and artistic creation."[32] In artistic creation the human being is for Ficino, as his disciple Francesco da Diacetto states, "truly the bond and knot of the universe."[33] As such, the human soul contains the higher without abandoning the lower. Humankind will ascend not by leaving the world behind but by including it.[34]

Human dignity gives to humans the task of reforming and re-creating the world. Individual and cosmos are so joined that to affirm the one is to affirm the other; it follows that the physical universe finds its best expression in the autonomous movements of the human mind in free creation.[35] Those elements of the universe that seem formless are to be given shape and form through human creativity, which involves the activities of scientist and artist alike.[36]

At this point the imagination, through art, explicitly enters the equation. Beauty becomes an element of human self-knowledge that arises in the creative act by which humankind imitates God.[37] Leonardo da Vinci puts this well when he states: "Oh investigator of things, do not praise yourself for your knowledge of things brought forth by nature in its natural course; rather enjoy knowing the aim and end of those things designed by your mind."[38] According to Leonardo, science is a re-creation through reason while art is a similar re-creation through imagination. Science and art are both basic expressions of humankind's making power as a created god.[39] And such making would essentially reflect humankind's integration with the cosmos and would be an individual expression of the whole. This notion of human expression as reflecting the whole leads to the third element of Renaissance thought I wish to highlight—eloquence.

Eloquence

Eloquence was the cultural ideal of the Renaissance.[40] In embracing it, the humanists were hearkening back to the Isocratean-Ciceronian tradition of well-formed language as a distinctive sign of a complete human nature and an essential condition of civic and social health.[41] As Jerry Seigal notes, both philosopher and rhetorician accepted the word *logos* as a distinguishing feature of the human condition, but "for the philosopher *logos* had the sense of *ratio*, reason, whereas for the orator it meant *oratio*, speech. To regard man primarily as a thinker was to posit different potentialities and expectations for him rather than to view him first of all as a speaker."[42]

This idea was neatly captured by Isocrates, who wrote that "eloquence . . . is the one endowment of our nature which singles us out from all living creatures, and by using this advantage we have risen above them in all other respects as well . . . for beautiful and accomplished speech is never allotted to ordinary men, but is the work of an intelligent mind."[43]

Under this ideal, *eloquentia*, or eloquence, was to be an expression of *sapientia*, or wisdom—and inseparable from it. Cicero's goal was to achieve a single sapientia that, holding within itself the knowledge of all human and divine things, expressed itself through eloquentia. The ideal was for eloquence to be what Cicero called "wisdom put into language."[44]

As an expression of human wisdom, eloquence had to be all-embracing; it had to address all aspects of human reality (especially the common and the mundane). As Grassi notes, "the problems of rhetoric hereby apply not merely to a special sphere of human existence but to every human activity and method of action."[45] An eloquent ordering of the human world proceeds by grasping the concrete and changing the *places* in which human beings find themselves: a grasping that proves to be valid when humans flourish in the context of the eloquent arrangement.[46] "In this way an understanding of language is formed that is distinguished from rationalistic logic because it stresses the primacy of language's historical character, dialectic, topics. From this it necessarily follows that 'genuine' language is rhetorical, imagistic, and metaphorical, since this is the only kind that is formed with reference to the particularly confined state of the listener in time and space."[47]

A speech made in such a language would be, in Cicero's terms, *ornatus*. In one sense, *ornatus* refers merely to "an adornment, decoration, embellishment."[48] But it also means "of the world," corresponding to the Greek word *kosmos*.[49]

Grassi notes that this usage refers ontologically to "the 'relationship' between particular parts and a whole and names the particular order that holds among them. The *ornatus*, therefore, is never something that belongs to particulars in isolation; only in relation to something else, a whole, does the particular receive its essential meaning and become part of an interconnected arrangement."[50] An *ornate* or *eloquent* speech is a speech of the *whole*. It is a speech "of the world."

Eloquence, then, was not conceived of as mere ornamentation, or as a series of verbal embellishments designed to stir the emotions of the untrained, as it has come to be commonly viewed today. Galileo seemed to best embody the modern view in the Renaissance. For him, necessity was the feature that most decisively separated nature from the arts. He relegates the arts to the realm of subjective fantasy, deeming only physical accounts of natural science truly objective.[51]

Galileo writes that "philosophy is written in the great book which ever lies before our eyes—I mean the universe—but we cannot understand it if we do not first learn the language . . . in which it is written. This book is written in the mathematical language."[52]

We can take Leonardo to represent the opposing view. Galileo basically agreed with Leonardo on nature, taking many of his views from him. But Leonardo would never have argued that art was subjectively arbitrary, insisting that artistic style (as an imaginative grasp of form) was as objective as any mathematical or scientific reasoning.[53] In humanist thought, according to Cassirer, Leonardo's insight was embodied in a new attitude toward form. And form was to be found not only in logic, mathematics, and science but in art and poetry as well. A concentration on form and style became one of the central motifs of Renaissance humanist thought: "One might say that nearly all the great achievements of the Renaissance are gathered here as in a focal point."[54]

This "feel" for form and style led Renaissance thinkers to try to "clarify" human expression, not in terms of abstract conceptual clarity and distinctness but in terms of the exact fantasy or the imaginative style appropriate to the discourse of the realm of human creativity.[55] An emphasis was placed on eloquentia as the quintessence of human genius, and its leading principles were to be found in oratory and rhetoric.[56] Leonardo stands as an emblem of the Renaissance resolution of the tension between imagination and nature in his insistence that fantasia as exact style reveals nature to humankind and is an instance of humanity's integration in nature.[57]

The idea of eloquence completes and epitomizes the elements of Renaissance thought that I have identified as essential to my narration of Vico's descent.[58] For eloquence essentially reflects the whole to which humanity is linked through its nature as a *mikrokosmos*, and it is a direct expression of the human maker's imagination as a created god. These elements illuminate Vico's rejection of the modern viewpoint and helped him begin his descent to the principles of humanity.

2 Eloquent Memory and Barbaric Clarity

Vico tells us in his *Autobiography* how he developed the principles of his new science out of a dialectical struggle with the growing trend
toward the mathematical model of knowledge. A key element in this
struggle was a recognition of the importance of imagination and memory in
contrast to the imageless and context-free inwardness of the method advocated by Descartes. What did Vico see as the key errors of the mathematical paradigm?

Imagination and Memory

According to Vico, he first began to understand the true import of
the mathematical paradigm through a study of the Latin poets. As he read
he came to the realization that the geometry of the ancients was something
suitable only for childhood—whether of the race or the individual—and
that an excessive immersion in its methodology, particularly in its algebraized form, was destructive of metaphysical analysis (*A* 123–125/12–
13). This is so because abstract geometry *confounds imagination and memory:* "Algebra sees only what is right under its eyes: memory is confounded,
since when the second sign is found algebra pays no further attention to the
first; imagination goes blind because algebra has no need of images" (*A*
125/12).

In following the mathematical paradigm man turns inward, rejecting the great truth of the principle of the microcosm: that we are integrated
through sensibility and imaginative creation with the world around us. As
Vico states in *Study Methods*, "Whenever the subject matter is unsuited to
deductive treatment, the geometric procedure may be a faulty or captious
way of reasoning" (*SM* 22/803).

In such a procedure, one level of human reality is exalted at the expense of other equally "valid" modes of experience, and man is disconnected from the living reality in which the truth is always the whole. "Listening not to me but the logos," states Heraclitus, "it is wise to agree that all things are one" (fr. 50).

But formal speech rejects the concrete integration of humans with their world through work and the arts, an integration that is expressed in the language of the *sensus communis*, or common sense. Ernesto Grassi writes that "in such a language we never meet with abstract human beings but rather with those who, like ourselves, find themselves through work, in temporal and spatial relationships. The concepts through which we come to understand and 'grasp' each situation come from our ingenious, metaphorical, fantastic capacities that convey meanings in the concrete situations with which we are confronted."[1] Under the Cartesian model man is no longer the knot and bond of the universe, uniting the lowest with the highest but is instead profoundly alone, existing in what Vico called "a deep solitude of spirit and will" (1106). According to Heraclitus, "Though the logos belongs to all, the many live as though they have a private understanding" (fr. 2). The logos that unites is the logos of the image.

The new mathematical paradigm also destroys the understanding in that "it professes to be divine" (*A* 125/13). The masters of abstraction are accused of forgetting that they are created gods. So they create for themselves a false microcosm in that they mistake one part of human reality for the whole, unintentionally re-creating in this way a false macrocosm bleached of image and eloquent speech.

The Cartesian seeks only the necessities of Galilean nature, ignoring the imperative of Ficino to reform the world through beauty and in this way come to self-knowledge. As Vico notes, "peoples who have reached this point of reflective malice . . . are sensible no longer of comforts, delicacies, pleasures and pomp, but only of the sheer necessities of life" (1106). In the inverted world of the mathematical paradigm, the patterns of inner abstraction give rise to an algebraized cosmos of extension in motion that gives the lie to the richly diverse forms of human life.

According to Grassi, rational speech under the mathematical paradigm, strictly considered, explains or infers only what its premises imply. This means that such speech is "monological in its deepest structure, for it is not bothered by emotion or place and time determinations in its rational process."[2]

It is *this* world that requires no study of rhetoric. It is *this* world that is the province of the dialect of intelligibility and clarity and distinctness—a backward province that despises eloquence through its mistaken identification of a part (however powerful a part) for the whole.

Making and Witnessing

With reality circumscribed through the denial of imagination and memory, the abstract mathematical thinker is in addition cut off from contact with divine providence, for human beings no longer picture themselves as making in the image of God (which cuts them off from the true roots of self-knowledge). Vico states that "the very form of our human mind . . . establishes the eternal idea as the principle of all things on the basis of the maker's knowledge and witnessing consciousness [*scienza e coscienza*] that we have of ourselves. In our mind there are certain eternal truths that we cannot mistake or deny, and which are therefore not of our own making. But for the rest we feel a liberty by thinking them to make all the things that are dependent on the body, and therefore we make them in time, that is, when we choose to turn our attention to them, and we make them all by thinking them and contain them all within ourselves" (*A* 127/14).

Here we see Vico distinguishing himself as a critical metaphysician from those, like Descartes, who lock themselves up within one mode of human making and thus fashion for themselves a prison from which there is no escape. In limiting themselves to criticism and ignoring topics, they have shut themselves out of the essential avenues of approach to the workings of the divine in history. These avenues are found in imagination and memory working through the clues that philology considers, and they are essentially concerned with time- and space-bound particulars.

We come to a witnessing consciousness (*coscienza*) of the divine only through the maker's knowledge (*scienza*) we have of ourselves as human beings. We can discover the realities not of our own making only through the conversion of *certa* (certains) into *vera* (trues), sifting in this way the human from the divine. When we remake the world in this way, we then begin to see those things we cannot truly appropriate but can only witness.

In turning from time- and space-bound particulars, the Cartesian metaphysician ironically isolates himself from the only possible route into the eternal ideas he so desperately seeks, which can be witnessed (not known) only through the conversion of the certain to the true as expressive of the workings of the ideal eternal history.

In the passage from the *Autobiography* cited above, Vico distinguishes between maker's knowledge and witnessing consciousness, *scienza* and *coscienza*. This distinction is to be understood in light of the principle discussed in *On the Ancient Wisdom of the Italians*, that "the true is precisely what is made." In this distinction we see Vico taking up the Renaissance principle of the human being as divine maker. And humans in their making imitate God, who, as the maker of all things, knows what he makes: "For God reads all the elements of things inner or outer, because He contains and disposes them in order, whereas the human mind . . . can never gather them all together" (*AW* 46/63).

Human beings likewise know only the things they make: "Just as divine truth is what God sets in order and creates in the act of knowing it, so human truth is what man puts together and makes in the act of knowing it. . . . By this very knowledge the mind makes the thing, because in knowing it puts together the elements of the thing" (*AW* 46/63). We have maker's knowledge, of those things we have made as human beings, such as mathematics or art, but we have only witnessing consciousness of things we are incapable of making, such as natural things (which have been made by God).

In this way we are "able to demonstrate geometrical propositions because we create them; were it possible for us to supply demonstrations of propositions of physics, we would be capable of creating them *ex nihilo* as well" (*SM* 23/803). Physics, in that its causes are to be found in God as maker, does not give us truths as does geometry but merely bears "a semblance of probability" (*SM* 23/803). But there can be a science of geometry, for in it "the true is precisely what is made" (*AW* 46/63). But in physics we have only consciousness of the objects in question, which are then not true but certain.

Vico began to recognize how science might become new when he realized that the world of civil society was made by human beings. He writes, in that most oft-quoted passage of the *Scienza nuova*, that "in the night of thick darkness enveloping the earliest antiquity, so remote from ourselves, there shines the eternal and never failing light of a truth beyond all question: that the world of civil society has certainly been made by men, and that its principles are therefore to be found within the modifications of our own human mind" (331).

In this passage we can see Vico combine the notion of the human being as microcosm and maker in a new way, in order to offer an avenue of approach to the civil whole with which humankind is integrated. It is true for Vico that we can never integrate ourselves with the natural world, as Ficino and other Renaissance thinkers believed. But it is not true, as Galileo and others maintained, that the only realm of necessary knowledge was the natural—in fact, these thinkers misunderstood the nature of our knowledge of nature and imputed to it a necessity it did not have.

According to Vico, "the criterion for possessing the science of something is being able to put it into effect, and proving from causes is making what one proves. And this being is absolutely true because it is convertible with the made and its cognition is identified with its operations" (*R* 167/156).

Under this criterion the situation becomes confused when the standards of mathematical knowledge—which as *made* things can be converted into maker's knowledge—are illegitimately applied to natural things, which cannot be so converted. Thus "the criterion of making what is known gives me the logical difference here: for in mathematics, I know the truth by making it; in physics and the other sciences, the situation is different" (*R* 167/156).

The Particular and the Eternal

The true route to necessary knowledge, in fact, lies through the very particulars, bound to time and place, that the modern paradigm of knowledge has come to ignore. The modern method always seeks to ascend, or abstract from the particular, either through inductive generalization or through intellectual insight into a thing's "essence" (think of Descartes and his example of the wax in *Meditations* II).

In so doing, however, the method misses the descent to the eternal, which is found through the particular: "Method is a good thing to discover when you can arrange the elements" (*R* 183/166). And Vico writes that "whoever reflects on this cannot but marvel that the philosophers should have bent all their energies to the study of the world of nature, which, since God made it, He alone knows; and that they should have neglected the study of the world of nations, or civil world, which, since men had made it, men could come to know" (331).

It is important here to distinguish between "the world of civil things" and "history." It is not Vico's view that humankind has made history in toto and that because human beings have made history, they can therefore know it. Vico is not a historicist. General axiom V states that "to be useful to the human race, philosophy must raise and direct weak and fallen man, not rend his nature or abandon him in corruption" (129). In the corollary Vico then notes that "this axiom dismisses from the school of our science the Stoics, who seek to mortify the senses, and the Epicureans, who make them the criterion. For both deny providence" (130).

But the route to the knowledge of providence is not found in an ascent from this world; as Vico notes in axiom VI, "philosophy considers man as he should be and so can be of service to but very few " (131). One must instead descend with jurisprudence to consider the human race as it is, seeing that "out of ferocity, avarice, and ambition, the three vices which run throughout the human race, it creates the military, merchant, and governing classes, and the strength, riches, and wisdom of the commonwealths" (132). In this way we see law making civil happiness out of destructive vice.

Descending, viewing humanity as it is, we can see that "there is a divine providence and further that it is a divine legislative mind. For out of the passions of men each bent on his own private advantage . . . it has made the civil institutions by which men may live in human society" (133). Though human beings make their civil things (*cose*), they do not make the history, the pattern that arises from human making in interaction with the divine.

It is true that the human being who creates in the image of God imitates God in converting the true with the made. But as Verene notes, "the principle that the true is the made is itself not made by man."[3] This means that human beings do not *make* the principles by which they can understand their humanity, but *find* them, for these principles define a humanity created by God.[4]

So there must be for Vico "a kind of *coscienza* or awareness of the divine that is presupposed and necessary for human *scienza*. This sense of *coscienza*, unlike that type of finding of the certain which takes place in philology or physics, and which holds the object at a distance, depends upon the ancient sense of imitation or *mimesis*. . . . The human being attempts to have access to its being by transforming its own being into an imitation of it and thereby discovering the divine being in its own created being."[5] Human beings always attempt to make history in imitation of the divine, the comprehension of which—in the sense of divine *scienza*—is always beyond their grasp.[6]

The Double Error

Thus history, according to Vico, contains within it a divine providence, an eternal order of ideas that human beings have not made but can only witness. Thinkers like Descartes, who have based their methods of inquiry on the abstract mathematical model, have thus involved themselves in a peculiar double error.

First, not understanding that the true is the made, these philosophers set up clarity and distinctness as a standard of truth. But what such thinkers hold to be clear and distinct are really only probable, and what they term clarity and distinctness are really only a function of *coscienza*. All they end up with is certainty, not truth.

Their situation calls to mind the saying of Jesus, "If the light that is in you is darkness, how great is that darkness" (Matt. 6:23), or, as Vico puts it, "knowing distinctly is a vice of the human mind" (*AW* 77/93). For in not realizing that the true is the made, these thinkers miss the appropriate standard of truth—eloquence—for they overlook the essential context of what is known.

Vico writes that when the human mind "knows a thing distinctly, it sees it by lamplight at night. For when the mind sees it thus, the thing's circumstances are lost from sight" (*AW* 77/93). In missing the context in this way, the Cartesian thinker also misses wisdom, which is essentially tied in with a sense of the whole.

Second, in not understanding human making, thinkers like Descartes also miss the phenomenon of divine making, for the two types of making must be reciprocally understood in the light of the principle of the microcosm and the created god. For it is when we act in God's image in the context of our integration with the world of civil things that we find providence through a *coscienza* of the divine.

This occurs because our making is inseparably bound up with the providential order in our nature as microcosm, and it enables us to be a witness to the workings of the divine in the light of human making, which depends in turn in its making on the divine. Vico states that "the very form of our human mind . . . establishes the eternal idea as the principle of all things on the basis of the maker's knowledge and witnessing consciousness that we have of ourselves" (*A* 127/14).

These two errors, then, show the Cartesian thinker to be utterly blinded to both the certain and the true found in human culture and history. For it is in culture and history that the topics (topoi) are to be found that guide Vico in the descent into his new science.

3 The Way Down

When Vico realized that the abstract mathematical mode of knowledge was the province of "minute wits," he was driven back into "the constant reading of orators, historians, and poets." And as he read, "his intellect took increasing delight in observing between the remotest matters ties that bound them together in some common relation" (A 123/12). Here, Vico points to a moment when he first began consciously to understand, as he states in the *New Science*, that philosophy must begin to "examine philology (that is, the doctrine of all the institutions that depend on human choice; for example, all histories of the languages, customs, and deeds of peoples in war and peace)" (7).

By this method one could take all the particular human creations and discover what binds them together, descending through human culture and history to "the form of a science by discovering in it the design of an ideal eternal history traversed in time by the histories of all the nations" (7). These ties, he notes, "are the beautiful ornaments of eloquence which make subtleties delightful" (A 123/12).

Such a procedure is necessarily and directly concerned with human memory, a methodological move that is the opposite of the methods of Cartesian science. Recall that in the *Autobiography* algebra was criticized because it had no need of memory; this had the further implication that imagination was confounded as well (A 123–126/12–14). For Vico, the true science of human knowing begins with remembering or recollecting the particular certains of human history found in the philological heritage.

But that memory could not be for Vico a mere collecting together of the various clear and distinct bits of knowledge we happen to find scattered throughout our past. Vico was no archæologist, and the history of ideas he offers is no mere intellectual history. Rather, he wishes to claim that "memory is the same as imagination" (819).

His science of memory, of a return to the origins, is based upon a different model of human remembering from the one commonly considered.

In his descent, Vico arrived at a different account of human making and knowing, which also restructured what he meant by memory. What did Vico mean by his claim that memory is the same as imagination? How does Vico understand memory, and how did he come to see it in this way?

The essential prelude to answering these questions is an understanding of Vico's discovery of the form taken by the thought of archaic humanity. What did Vico discover about how the first humans thought that laid a radically new epistemological foundation for his new science? What was the "nature or birth [*natura o nascimento*]" (148) of the "commencing of truly human thinking" (6)? How did human thinking come into being (*nascimento*), and at what time and in what guise (147)?

The Master Key

Vico notes in the section on method in the *New Science* that in order to determine answers to questions such as these we must begin where our subject begins, in "the time these creatures began to think humanly" (338). Previous attempts to understand the origins of humankind failed through not following a guiding principle of metaphysics, which is that metaphysical thought must seek "its proofs not in the external world but within the modifications of the mind who meditates it. For since this world of nations has certainly been made by men, it is within these modifications that its principles should have been sought" (374).

Note here that Vico calls not for introspection but for attention to the civil world rather than the world of nature. In this way metaphysics can return to true and knowable beginnings. And human beings in their beginnings were bounded by sense, which was their "sole way of knowing things" (6). Not being able to think abstractly or to form "intelligible class concepts," the rough and savage creatures of human beginnings then "had a natural need to create poetic characters; that is, imaginative class concepts or universals" (209).

The discovery that the first peoples were "by a demonstrated necessity of nature . . . poets who spoke in poetic characters," Vico calls "the master key of this science." He states that these poetic characters are "imaginative genera"—images formed by the imagination to which all the species or particulars of a genus are reduced. These imaginative genera are "true fables or myths" that are found to contain "not analogical but univocal" meanings (34). He adds to his definition that these "first theological poets," as the founders of humanity, made as their "first divine fable, the greatest they ever created: that of Jove, king and father of men and gods, in the act of hurling the lightning bolt" (379). The first poets thus "founded the gentile nations with fables of the gods" (7).

What was the need out of which these poetic characters were created? What does it mean that the first human beings were bounded by sense and could not think in intelligible class concepts? What does it mean that imaginative genera are true fables with univocal meanings? Why were the first poets theological—their first fable a divine one, of Jove? And how did this first fable become extended throughout the world, so that the first nations were founded by the fables of the gods?[1]

Poetic Chaos

When the theological poets consider "physics," Vico tells us, they consider the world of nations (688). Their method is in keeping with the guiding principle of metaphysics noted above, that its proofs not be sought in the natural world. And when the theological poets envisioned the experience of chaos from which they emerged, they did so under the aspect of three poetic characters: Orcus, Pan, and Proteus.

Orcus was the monster who devoured all things, as humans were devoured and deprived of their proper form through the uncertainty of their offspring, existing in "the confusion of human seeds." Pan was a monstrous figure who roamed the dark forest, ranging through it as the "potential humans" did, because "there was no institution of humanity [*ordine d'umanità*] in it." All was chaos and Panlike confusion because "men in this infamous promiscuity did not have the proper form of men," being "impious vagabonds wandering through the great forests of the earth and having the appearance of men but the habits of abominable beasts." And finally Proteus, the shape-changer, represents the nature of those not-yet humans, "who (just as children, looking in a mirror, will try to seize their own reflections) thought from the various modifications of their own shapes and gestures that there must be a man in the water, forever changing into different shapes" (688).

These potential human beings existed in both a civil and an epistemological flux, unable to orient themselves and thus generate and produce "in themselves the proper human form" in either a civil or an individual sense (692). Vico notes that we can scarcely comprehend such a condition, "for their minds were so limited to particulars that they regarded every change of facial expression as a new face . . . and for every new passion . . . a new heart" (700).

These creatures existed in a continual flux; their minds "took things one at a time, being in this respect little better than the minds of beasts, for which each new sensation cancels the last one (which is the cause of their being unable to compare and reason discursively)" (703). In the words of Heraclitus, "It scatters . . . and gathers. . . . It comes together and flows away. . . . It approaches and departs" (fr. 9).

The flux was the original chaos, out of which order was formed—the original condition of primal human need. As time passed, more abstract and refined metaphysicians, controlled by their arrogance or conceit (*boria*), and not understanding the task of metaphysics to be the contemplation of the modifications of the human mind, transferred these real and humanly understandable beginnings into the natural chaos of "the universal seeds of nature" (688).

Therefore, these scholars made over the "true and severe" account of the poets into something more esoteric and sublime, the chaos of Orcus, for example, being taken to mean "the prime matter of natural things, which, formless itself, is greedy for forms and devours all forms," while Proteus became "first matter," which is potentially all forms and shapes (688).

In this way, blinded by their conceits, the last human beings, the moderns, make "sublime learning" out of the simplicity of the first human beings, who were under the spell of immediacy (688). As Verene notes, "immediacy is the state of pure particularity in which each moment is new, in which there is no place, no [topos] for thought. . . . This immersion in the particular in which one appearance or perception follows the other without the achievement of meaning is a nullity, a kind of nothingness."[2] And as Vico states, peoples "in that human indigence . . . were almost all body and no reflection" (819). They were "unable to compare and reason discursively" (703).

One might almost say these first creatures existed in a state of nonbeing. How are we to understand intelligibility emerging from this chaotic flux? And how is this emerging intelligibility to be understood in comparison with reflective or discursive thought?

Intelligibility

How do intelligible universals organize human experience? According to Vico, they essentially abstract from the particular: their truth thus becomes "a formula devoid of any particular form" (1045). Intelligible universals form the basis of abstract thought and are for this reason also known as abstract universals (1040). They are the universals of ordinary logic.

Vico sees the abstract universal in its current form as beginning to develop in the West with Socrates. This conforms to his notion that the latest achievements of thought "in metaphysics, logic, and morals" represent a *devolution* "from the marketplace of Athens" (1043). When Socrates observed Athenian citizens enact laws through agreement "in an idea of equal utility common to all of them severally," he must have begun "to adumbrate intelligible genera or abstract universals by induction" (1040).

This foreshadowing of abstract universals occurred when Socrates collected the "uniform particulars which go to make up a genus of that in respect of which the particulars are uniform among themselves" (1040). In this way Socrates founded our epoch and inaugurated the age of the barbarism of reflection. And the thrust of any such thinking is the same in its beginnings: "As the mind moves to higher and higher levels of specific and generic abstraction, the particular position of the individual entity is lost."[3] Everything loses its place.

But the first humans were bounded by the flux of sense. In their situation there was no experience from which to abstract an ordering principle for a series of objects, for there are no objects to make up the series; no possibility for a series of events when there are as of yet no "events."

One is *unable* to rise from "the perception of individual objects to the essential properties that constitute them as species and to the generic ordering of the species by omitting sensuous content for the original perceptions, so the mind can descend from genus to species to individual object by adding elements of specific content."[4] For there is no "perception of individual objects" fundamentally *given* to human knowing. How then did intelligibility arise for the first human beings?

According to Vico, the first humans, driven by the indigence of their lot, created in response to their situation not abstractions but "certain models or ideal portraits," to which they reduced "all the particular species which resembled them" (209). They did this because "the human mind is naturally impelled to take delight in uniformity" (204). So the first humans created meaning through master images as ideal portraits, *fables*, which then became the criteria of what was real: "These fables are ideal truths suited to the merit of those of whom the vulgar tell them; and such falseness to fact as they contain consists simply in failure to give their subjects their due. So that, if we consider the matter well, poetic truth is metaphysical truth, and physical truth which is not in conformity with it should be considered false" (205).

Such thinking has its own internal sense of order and coherence— its own "poetic logic" (400). As Verene notes, "for Vico the poetic character, or fable, occupies the same central position in poetic (mythic) thought which the generic concept occupies in rational (modern) thought."[5] And according to Vico's analysis, the term *logic* comes from *logos*, "whose first and proper meaning was *fabula*, fable" (401). The fable, the poetic character, then, makes the world a human reality; it makes the original experience of which discursive thought is a pale abstraction. Vico states that "the first age invented the fables to serve as true narratives" (808), that is, "the fables in their origins were true and severe narrations, whence *mythos*, fable, was defined as *vera narratio*" (814).

That the fables constitute the criteria of reality for the mythic mentality explains why "the principle of the true poetic allegories . . . gave univocal, not analogical meaning for various particulars comprised under their poetic genera" (210). This means that a particular is not thought of in an analogical sense as being *like* an ideal portrait but that the individual cannot be thought of apart from it: he or she *is* it.[6]

Vico cites as examples the characters of Achilles and Odysseus, who sum up respectively (as we might say) all the properties of heroic valor and heroic wisdom for the Greek people (809). But a brave man is not, for the mythic mentality, *like* Achilles, and the wise man is not *like* Odysseus; the brave man *is* Achilles, the wise man *is* Odysseus (403).[7] Thus "the distinctive characteristic of mythic . . . thought is its power to assert identities, not similarities."[8] Or as Vico puts it, the true war chief is the one the poet invents, "and all the chiefs who do not conform themselves throughout to Godfrey are not true chiefs of war" (205).

Such thinking is indeed hard to enter into or conceive of, as Vico constantly reminds us. Owen Barfield notes that the minds of children (a favorite Vichian clue) can help us understand the ancient mentality (if we avoid the pitfalls of arrogance and conceit).[9] As Barfield points out, "the adult observer constantly misreads his own logical processes into the child's mind" when the "child's apparent generalizations are in reality single meanings, which it has not yet learnt to split up into two or more."[10] Although for the child every man is "Papa," the child is not using the *Papa* to express a general idea like *man*, for "the child has no such general idea. He has one single meaning, 'papa.'"[11]

Support for this analysis can be found in Willard Quine's analysis of "mass terms," which he calls the "archaic survival of the first phase of language learning."[12] In attempting to clarify how abstract thinking evolves from singular and general terms, Quine posits a stage of thought that is psychologically and epistemologically prior to the stage that uses general terms. This earlier stage is characterized by the use of such mass terms as *water, red,* or *Mama,* which do not designate discrete objects.

Quine writes that we "in our maturity" view the child's mother as an integral object that irregularly orbits the child, occasionally revisiting it; while red is something quite different, existing as generally scattered about. Water is somewhere between red and mother—scattered about, but still "stuff."[13] But for the child, *mother, red,* and *water* are all the same: "a history of sporadic encounter" totally different from "our adult conceptual scheme of mobile enduring objects, identical from time to time and place to place."[14]

Quine goes on to show how general and singular terms, predication, and abstract terms arise out of this stage of conceptual development. He notes that "we have in these reflections some materials for speculations regarding the early beginnings of an ontology of attributes in the childhood of the race . . . that the attributes are vestiges of the minor deities of some creed outworn."[15]

Quine would apparently agree with Barfield that for mythic thinking, objects "were not, as they appear to be at present, isolated, or detached, from thinking and feeling."[16] Archaic thinking was then, as Vico has it, "not in the least abstract, refined, or spiritualized, because [the first human beings] were entirely immersed in the senses, buffeted by the passions, buried in the body" (378). The myth of Demeter and Persephone, to use Barfield's example, does not represent an attempt to explain why it is darker in winter than in summer. Ancient human beings did not notice recurring instances of phenomena over the seasons and then propose to themselves myths, like that of Demeter, as some sort of bush-league hypotheses. Ancient human beings were, as Quine might put it, too lost in "confusions over mass terms, confusions of sign and object, perhaps even a savage theology" for that.[17] Instead, we find in the myth "the ideas of waking and sleeping, of summer and winter, of life and death, of mortality and immortality all lost in one pervasive meaning."[18] Demeter *is* what poetic wisdom faces in confronting the forces of nature, providing orientation in the buffeting flux. Through the myth human beings achieve primary orientation or *place*.

Vico states that the flux of humanity was first stayed by a poetic apprehension of the thundering sky. "Then," he writes, "on certain occasions ordained by divine providence (occasions which our science studies and discovers), shaken and aroused by a terrible fear, each of the particular Uranus and Jove he had feigned and believed in, some of them finally left off wandering and went into hiding in certain places" (13).

The "idea" of the thundering sky, shaped not by reasoning but by the senses (502), became the first human thought in the midst of the flux. In the Quinean dialect, one might call this the first *occasion sentence* of the human race, giving rise to the first real stimulus meaning; what one might call the *primary occasion sentence* of humanity. What does it mean that a thought is shaped by the senses? What could it mean that the first human beings thought with their bodies in establishing the origins (*archai*) of the human world?

A Metaphysics of the Body

In his "Final Corollaries concerning the Logic of the Learned," in chapter VII of Book II of the *Scienza nuova*, Vico notes that "the first founders of humanity applied themselves to a sensory topics" (495). As traditionally understood, topics related to the notion of having a "mental place" from which to draw forth arguments (a subject to which I shall devote considerable space in Chapter 5).[19]

A sensory topics concerns itself, not with the formulation of arguments but with the formulation of the human world. It deals with the original power of the poetic mind to orient itself in the primordial flux; to "hew out" a place (*dirozzare la topica*) in the forest of humanity's formlessness (497). A sensory topics is interested in understanding how a mind has experience: how there *is* something rather than *nothing* that the mind is capable of experiencing.[20]

In occupying itself with a sensory topics, Vico tells us, "the first age of the world occupied itself with the primary operation of the human mind" (496). The mind is primarily concerned with the foundation of the "is"; the real, which stands under, supports, and orients the human in its being. Verene notes that "the carrying of particular sensation to a fixed place or universal of sense . . . is the appearance of *is* in experience. . . . In the imaginative universal something *is* for the mind."[21]

The metaphysics that achieves this knowledge of being, however, is very different from the abstract metaphysics of the modern age of philosophical thought. For the "rough and crude" metaphysics of the first human beings involves itself with true knowledge, and thus with *making the is*; recall that for Vico *verum esse ipsum factum*—the true is the same as the made. The first metaphysicians thus created the being they knew, or they later understood it by means of a descent through the modifications of the human mind to that primordial making. Theirs is a metaphysics of the senses, a metaphysics of the body. The sky thunders, and the savage creature as newly born metaphysician shakes, beginning to think humanly by thinking as a bodily being. This was a time, as Barfield notes, when humans were "conscious in the beating of their hearts and the pulsing of their blood—when thinking was not merely *of* Nature, but was Nature herself."22

The first human thought is the actual shaking of the body; the second thought the actual running into the cave and remaining there. Vico states that husbands "shared their first human idea with their wives, beginning with the idea of a divinity which compelled them to drag their women into their caves; and thus even this vulgar metaphysics began to know the human mind in God" (506). It was the physical act of dragging the women into the cave and compelling them to remain there that was in fact the "thought" they were sharing! As the two dwelt in the cave, a second thought was born, one of Juno, or marriage.

Such "thoughts" were what Vico calls "truths of the senses," which were spoken mutely, in a language of gestures and movements. "The thunderous motion of the sky that covers the world like a ceiling sweeps over the heads of the *giganti* whose bodies involuntarily tremble in imitation of the celestial motion. The motion instilled in their bodies becomes the quasi-mental motion of the gesture, the half-voluntary movements that fix their sensations on a difference between the conditions of the earth and sky."23

In this way, as Heraclitus notes, "Thunderbolt steers all things" (fr. 64). Under the aegis of the thunderbolt, humans began to hew out their humanity in hewing out a place in the world. Humanity and the world arise together out of the chaos, for the only real world we can know is the human. And that world is one to which we are linked as microcosm to macrocosm; to found humanity is to found the world.

With this account Vico gives us a genuine metaphysics of the body. In the beginning (*en archē*) humans thought as bodily creatures, and this archē is the governing root of human thought. No matter what stage of refinement or dissolution human thought reaches, it is ruled by this governing root, and is in some sense related to it.

Consider, for example, how "being" was understood in such a metaphysics; a concept that, when reflectively understood, is "most abstract, as transcending all particular beings" (693). But the theological poets "understood being quite grossly in the sense of eating," for *being* equals *subsisting*, "just as when our peasants want to say that a sick man lives [i.e., has not died] they say he still eats" (693). The barbarism of reflection is a kind of perversion of the body; the body turns against itself and denies itself as it goes mad and wastes its substance.

I have shown how the first human thought was a physical act; how the shaking of fear *was* that thought. Subsequent ideas, such as of Juno, or marriage, are then to be understood in the same way: as the actual remaining in the cave with one woman out of sight of the thundering sky. The "remaining" was marriage, and it was lived and understood and communicated through the senses and the body. Other forms of human thought are continuous with this. How are we to understand the logic of this type of thinking?

A Logic of the Senses

The language of the first humans "was a fantastic speech making use of physical substances endowed with life" (401). Early humans apprehended Jove, Cybele, and Neptune, for example, by mutely pointing, understanding them "as substances of the sky, the earth, and the sea, which they imagined to be animate divinities and were therefore true to their senses in believing them to be gods" (402). In this way the human world was created in the image of the body, attributing senses and passions to bodies "as vast as the sky, sea, and earth" (402). Barfield notes that this is "a kind of thinking which is at the same time perceiving—a picture thinking, a figurative, or imaginative consciousness, which we can only grasp today by true analogy with the imagery of our poets, and to some extent, with our own dreams."[24]

Vico understands the form of such thinking in his poetic logic through the notion of the first tropes, or primary modes of expression, that are found in rhetorical theory: metaphor, metonymy, synechdoche, and irony. And the last, irony, is not a poetic trope but a trope of the age of reflection.[25] But Vico does not understand the first three tropes as referring to an abstract language, a refined grammar of terms, as they have come to be understood through reflection, but as relating to the original language of the body which the first men "spoke." What can it mean to consider the logic of the forms of bodily thought?

According to Vico, "that which is metaphysics insofar as it contemplates things in all the forms of their being, is logic insofar as it considers things in all the forms by which it may be signified. Accordingly, as poetry has been considered . . . as a poetic metaphysics in which the theological poets imagined bodies to be for the most part divine substances, so now . . . [it] is considered as poetic logic" (400). The forms of logic are the forms of the master images or fables Vico will study in the light of the first tropes. The primary trope, in Vico's view, is metaphor, which for him is the agent of identity and being. We may take the metaphor's relation to bodily logic as a way to understand the others as well.

As Vico writes, "the most luminous and therefore the most necessary and frequent" trope is metaphor (404). A metaphor based upon the metaphysics of the body, however, is quite different from one based upon the metaphysics of reflection. The metaphors "spoken" by the first men are based upon *identity*, not *likeness:* Jove is not like the thundering sky, he *is* the thundering sky, apprehended in shaking and flight.

Metaphor creates truth and reality; it is not an abstraction or an observation but a true act of original *poiēsis*. It "gives sense and passion to insensate things," endowing them with "the being of animate substances," and so makes fables of them (404). A metaphor as understood in poetic logic through the metaphysics of the body does not interpret experience but creates it. Vico calls this metaphor a "fable in brief" (404). As such it is an image that fixes sensation into a "true speech." In this particular master image, then, the necessity of the whole is found again. Universality is achieved through the particular, which brings forth the "is" as a human given.[26]

Through such creative tropes as these, "the first founders of humanity applied themselves to a sensory topics, by which they brought together those properties or qualities or relations of individuals and species which were, so to speak, concrete, and from these created their poetic genera" (495). Every metaphor understood in this way becomes the most basic element of human epistemology and the basis for human logic (logic being here understood as a "logic of life"). It was the act of "invention" in the first times that allowed for the "demonstration" of "all things necessary to human life" (498).

Rational demonstration is unconnected with concrete situations. As Ernesto Grassi notes, the language of rational demonstration is *apodictic:* "it shows something (*deiknumi:* I show) upon (*apo*) the basis of reasons. It cannot be bound to times, places, or personalities; it is *unrhetorical*."[27] Since such language is monologically deductive, "its essence is such that it can possess *no* 'inventive' character."[28] Demonstration in the purely rational sense, then, is fundamentally sterile.

Archaic logic is fecund; it involves a "creative showing" through the original poiēsis of founding metaphor. And if such speech is a "showing" that points toward the concrete situation, then it is also necessarily figurative or imagistic.[29] This means, as Grassi points out, that such thinking is truly "theoretical" (from *theorein*, "to see"). It is thus metaphorical: "it shows something which has a sense, and this means that to the figure, to that which is shown, the speech transfers [*metapherein*] a signification; in this way the speech which realizes this showing 'leads before the eyes' [*phainesthai*] a significance. This speech is and must be in its structure an imaginative language."[30] Metaphor is the primary operation of the human mind in the noetic act.[31]

In such knowing, the principle of verum esse ipsum factum becomes, as Verene notes, the inner working of the imaginative universal, "because, through the image, which is the metaphor understood on this level, the primary act of intelligibility takes place."[32] Jove is, of course, the primary example of this, for "every gentile nation had its Jove" (193).

As the first human thought, Jove is what Verene terms a "total name," because it proves to be a fixed point that has reference to the total flux. Only through the divine can the whole be rediscovered "in the negative time of the flux, the original motion that lacks place."[33] The total name *divides* the flux into earth and sky, providing a topos for bodily movement (that equals human thought).[34]

For Vico the operation of the archaic metaphor in human knowing "is a consequence of our axiom that man in his ignorance makes himself the rule of the universe, for in the examples cited [of metaphoric making] he has made of himself an entire world" (405). The primary act of human noetic poiēsis is rooted in ignorance. And ignorance is also intimately connected with a knowledge of the whole through the microcosm principle of being human. What can it mean to say that human beings truly know only through ignorance? And that only through ignorance can we gain knowledge of the whole?

In explaining human knowing, Vico contrasts rational metaphysics with imaginative. "Rational metaphysics teaches that man becomes all things by understanding them" while "imaginative metaphysics shows that man becomes all things by *not* understanding them." For when man understands, "he extends his mind and takes in things," but when he does not, "he makes the things out of himself and becomes them by transforming himself into them" (405).

This type of knowledge is what Vico called in *Ancient Wisdom* "a metaphysics compatible with human frailty" (*AW* 109/131). Based upon the principle that verum esse ipsum factum, it recognizes that the human being as microcosm makes in the image of God but not as God. And since God made the world, God knows it, while human beings merely witness it. Humankind does not have a metaphysical knowledge of the world, which is always a knowledge from causes, that is, from being the maker.

In *Ancient Wisdom* Vico discussed how humankind did, in fact, make an intellectual world on the model of God, as if from nothing, in creating mathematics. In this case the human mind, like God, contains "the elements of the truths that it can order and compose; and it is through the disposition and composition of these elements that the truth they demonstrate arises; so that demonstration is the same as construction, and the true is the same as the made" (*AW* 65/83).

In the *Scienza nuova* Vico comes to see that the world of nations was made by human beings; that our basic orientation as human beings in the midst of a nature we cannot really know is based upon topoi constructed through archaic metaphor as the primary operation of the human mind. We cannot know the nature we are in the midst of per causas, for we do not contain its causes within ourselves. But this reality of not knowing the created world, this primal indigence, drives us to remake it—to make human or civil things out of ourselves, through transforming ourselves into them. We can come to know these things per causas, and out of profound ignorance we can gain scienza, maker's knowledge, of a very human whole.

The ignorance of the first humans was what Vico calls a "simplicity" (408). They had what we might call simple ignorance, in contrast to the dissolute ignorance of the last moderns. It is this dissolute ignorance that gives rise to the double conceit of nations and scholars (120–138). Verene notes that Vico's first four axioms, which diagnose the basic human tendency toward boria, offer an account not of simple ignorance but of how ignorance becomes arrogance. [35]

The simple ignorance of the first humans and how they thought through imagination rather than discursive intellect becomes hidden through the inveterate tendency toward making over the unfamiliar into the familiar. Vico hopes to overcome this through the learned ignorance of his new science. [36] This is an ignorance that knows, along with Heraclitus, that "You would not find out the boundaries of the soul, even by marching over every road, so deep a logos does it have" (fr. 45).

Such an ignorance would enable us to counteract our tendencies toward the degenerative ignorance of the moderns and enable us, through *fantasia*, to descend to the "deep logos" of the unfamiliar. If we cannot encounter the unfamiliar as something *strange*, Barfield notes, we shall be able to think only as collectors rather than remakers of meaning through the maker's imagination. [37] One knows that one has encountered the truly unfamiliar when the strangeness has "an interior significance; it must be felt as arising from a different plane or mode of consciousness, and not merely as eccentricity of expression. It must be a strangeness of *meaning*." [38] One must be able to recognize the other, and salute it as such, through the art of unthinking the obvious. [39]

Barfield states that such a sense of unfamiliarity or strangeness is not the same as wonder, which is merely our reaction to things we do not rationally understand. [40] Strangeness instead has a contrary effect, arising "from contact with a different kind of *consciousness* from our own, different, yet not so remote that we cannot partly share it, as indeed, in such a connection, the mere word *contact* implies."[41] To encounter such strangeness we must unthink the obvious, resisting the human tendency to convert the unfamiliar into the familiar. According to Heraclitus, "If we do not expect the unexpected we shall not find it out, since it unsearchable and hard to see our way through" (fr. 18).

4 The Way Up

In commenting on the mode of knowledge operative in the *Scienza nuova*, Vico says that "as geometry, when it constructs the world of quantity out of its elements, or contemplates the world, is creating it for itself, just so does our Science create for itself the world of nations, but with a reality greater by just so much as the things having to do with human affairs are more real than points, lines, surfaces, and figures are. And this very fact is an argument, O reader, that these proofs are of a kind divine and should give thee a divine pleasure, since in God knowledge and creation are one and the same thing" (349).

Here one created god speaks to another of the knowledge of the whole, the wisdom, that arises from the logic of learned ignorance. How are we to understand this from the perspective of the *New Science* itself? Given a knowledge of how the first humans thought, a realization per causas of the beginnings of human reality, what are we to make of the resultant form of knowledge? What happens when we remake the making of the first created gods into a truth for ourselves in the age we live in?

Owen Barfield notes of a similar concern: "It must be remembered that it is just a part of the point at issue that reality is *not* susceptible of direct expression in modern language. Thus, the meaning . . . is accessible only to the active imagination of the reader himself, if he has good will enough to try and reconstruct, on the basis of what is given," these realities.[1] How do we remember the realities of these origins and remake them into a known whole?

The Problem of Memory

Vico's scienza is a science of *origins;* it requires that we remember the beginnings of humanity through the modifications of the human mind. Here the development of the individual and that of civilization can again give us a clue (as it did when we looked at the mentality of the child to understand the mentality of the first human beings). Barfield asks us to consider "the way in which the child's experience can acquire poetic value *as remembered* by the conscious, full-grown man. The old, single, living meanings which the individual, like the race, splits up and so kills, as he grows, are allowed to impinge *as memory* on the adult consciousness. . . . This is the true sense in which the child is father of the man."[2]

But this involves a problem for both the race and the individual, for the adult's consciousness is not like the child's; and the very concern of the adult to record and remember arises in tandem with that same changed consciousness that finds it hard to comprehend what is worth remembering.[3] We become rational, forgetting the very experience which structures that which we would remember. As individuals, we look for ideas, generated through induction based on observation of the discrete events of our personal history, in the same way that scholars examine the childhood of the human race; seeking analogies, we are unable to identify ourselves with the living principles of archaic mentality.[4] We cannot become a child, just as we cannot become one of the first humans. We face the problem of memory: "How, and in what form, to carry over into the uninspired *self*-consciousness some *memory* of that other inspired consciousness, which to the unpoetic man is not consciousness at all but sleep."[5]

Throughout the *Scienza nuova* Vico continually emphasizes the difficulty of recapturing the mentality of the first humans. He notes in the section on poetic metaphysics that "the nature of our civilized minds is so detached from the senses, even in the vulgar, by abstractions corresponding to all the abstract terms our language abounds in," that it is "beyond our power to enter into the vast imaginations of those first men" (378). He states that "we can scarcely understand, still less imagine, how these first men thought [ch'or appena intender si può, affatto immaginar non si può, come pensassero i primi uomini]" (378). In the section on method he points out that the first humans thought in a manner "which we cannot at all imagine and can comprehend only with great effort [le quali ci è affatto niegato d'immaginare e solamente a gran pena ci è permesso d'intendere]" (338). And in the section on poetic physics he again claims, "We can scarcely understand and cannot at all imagine how the first men thought [ch'or intender appena si può, affatto immaginar non si può come pensassero i primi uomini]" (700).

In these passages, Vico notes how human beings whose thought and imagination are structured by abstract universals cannot really comprehend the thought of the first human beings, which is structured by the imaginative universal. The key here is the term *imagination*. As Verene notes, Vico carefully uses the Italian word *immaginare*. In English, two different words, *fantasia* and *immaginazione*, are translated as "imagination." But the one is quite different from the other for Vico.[6]

Immaginazione is a faculty of the age of rational abstraction, limited to the Cartesian flatness of *coscienza*. It can only witness, not remake, and thus comprehends from the outside in two-dimensional flatness. Thus modern human beings "cannot at all imagine [*immaginare*]" the mentality of the first humans, for they would need to remake that mentality to have a maker's knowledge (scienza) of it (700).[7]

If one is to have a science of origins that recollects the *archai* of human thought, it must be sought for in a way different from *coscienza*-bound cognition. Verene notes that "for the *verum-factum* principle to function in the *New Science* we must be able to make our way back in some way to the origin of human thought and activity and we must be able to do this in a way as to remake the human world as something true for us . . . seeing the origin of humanity as *our* origin."[8]

This means, as Barfield notes, a return to the same principle of the making of meaning that is operative in the archaic mentality. And this, in line with the principles of true metaphysics, is to be found in the modifications of the human mind: "The same creative activity, once operative in meaning without man's knowledge or control, and only recognized long afterwards, when he awoke to contemplate, as it were, what he had written in his sleep, this is now to be found within his own consciousness."[9] How are we to understand a memory that remakes meaning? What is the structure of such a memory?

Memoria

Vico states in *Study Methods* that abstract philosophical criticism benumbs the imagination and stupefies the memory, "whereas poets are endowed with surpassing imagination, and their immanent spirit is Memory" (*SM* 42/817). He thus links imagination and memory, further noting of memory that it, "though not exactly the same as imagination, is almost identical with it" (*SM* 14/799). We saw that Vico makes the same claim in the *Scienza nuova*, that "la memoria è la stessa che la fantasia [memory is the same as the maker's imagination]" (819). He also notes in axiom L that "la fantasia . . . altro non è che memoria o diltata o composta [the maker's imagination is nothing but extended or compounded memory]" (211).

These two passages about fantasia are to be held in contrast to the three passages regarding immaginazione cited above. For immaginazione is precisely the "benumbed imagination" of which *Study Methods* spoke; the imagination which "goes blind," as Vico says in the *Autobiography*, resulting in the fact that "memory is confounded" (*A* 125/13). What exactly is this faculty that abstract thinking so restricts?

Vico states in the *Scienza nuova* that "memory has three different aspects: memory when it remembers things, a maker's imagination, when it alters or imitates them, and invention when it gives them a new turn or puts them into proper arrangement or relationship [ch'è memoria, mentre rimembra le cose; fantasia, mentre l'altera e contrafà; ingegno, mentre le contorna e pone in acconezza ed assettamento]" (819) MEMORIA thus comprises *memoria*, *fantasia*, and *ingegno*.

In the mentality of the first humans, MEMORIA operated to collect the world together into a human place. The three kinds of memory operated as a whole in the functioning of the imaginative universal as it made the human world. To explain these three aspects of MEMORIA with respect to the thinking of the first humans and the functioning of the imaginative universal, I shall examine each in turn, before turning to consider their parallel functioning in Vico's new science.

Memoria, mentre rimembra le cose. Memory in this sense is not a collective term for the three aspects of MEMORIA, but a type of MEMORIA.[10] It is simply the power to recall something, *rimembrare*. According to Verene, "*memoria*, as part of the structure of the imaginative universal, occurs at the point where a moment is fixed within the self-canceling flux of sensation."[11] It first occurred when thunder and fear became the image-based thought of Jove; when sensation first became thought. Remembering in this sense concerns the construction of a moment of identity through metaphor; the ability to return again and again to the same topos.[12]

Fantasia, mentre l'altera e contrafà. MEMORIA is called the maker's imagination when it alters and imitates. According to Verene, fantasia as memory is the ability to reorder what has been recalled (that is, fixed as image through metaphor) in simple memory and shape it in a human way: "The power to give the object distinctively human form."[13] Here we can recall the lesson of learned ignorance, that "man" becomes all things through not understanding them, because then "he makes the things out of himself and becomes them by transforming himself into them" (405). Fantasia alters and imitates through constantly returning to the image, shaping it into a human re-presentation. In this way it allows the human being to encounter the unfamiliar as something strange that yet has meaning.[14] Through fantasia we can contact the unfamiliar and make it our own; it is the only route of escape from the circle of conceit which constricts reality to our image.

In terms of the structure of the imaginative universal, the immediate recollection of simple memory "is actually moved by *fantasia* into the medium of the subject."[15] Jove is found again in the human body, for the ability to reexperience Jove slowly evolves into the world of human culture and language, which exist as traces or footprints of the archaic maker's imagination.[16] Memory deals with *cose*—the civil things that humans make. Fantasia takes the given identity of simple memory that stays the flux, and extends or compounds it into a human world: "la fantasia . . . altro none è che memoria o diltata o composta" (211). The "is" of identity, the simple being of place and orientation, is compounded, remade into the cose, the cultural institutions of the human world.

Ingegno, mentre le contorna e pone in acconezza ed assettamento. Bergin and Fisch translate "mentre le contorna" as "when it gives them a new turn" (819). There are several other senses to *contornare* that can bring out the meaning of *ingegno* in even more depth. *Contornare* also means "to surround; to go round; to outline; to border."[17] A *contorno* can be an "outline" or "ornamental border"; and, in the plural, "surroundings" or "environment."[18]

Vico states in *Ancient Wisdom* that "ingenium is the faculty that connects disparate and diverse things" (*AW* 96/117). It does this through *framing* one image in its relation to another, *outlining* in this way a master context of the whole. Ingegno "goes round" the primary sensory topics, creating the human "surroundings" or "environment" by "noting the commonplaces that must all be run over in order to know all there is in a thing that one desires to know well; that is, completely" (497). It environs the human world.

Ingegno is the faculty that allowed Vico to observe, as he notes in the *Autobiography*, "between the remotest matters, ties that bound them together in some common relation" (*A* 123/12). Ingegno thus establishes an "ornamental border," an eloquent framing of the whole: "It is these ties that are the beautiful ornaments of eloquence which make subtleties delightful" (*A* 123/12). Ingegno knits the archaic topics into a beautiful whole.

In terms of the structure of the imaginative universal, Verene notes that ingegno is related to the power of the *name*, which is realized in one shattering instant; when naming one thing leads to the naming of all things in an interconnected whole. After Jove is named, the world becomes full of gods. As the sensory topoi are connected, an interconnected whole arises in which one act of meaning implicates all others.[19]

Through MEMORIA the first human beings collected a human world. The *Scienza nuova* purports to re-collect what these first humans gathered. That which is recollected in this way is a whole reformed and remade through fantasia. What is the shape of this whole?

Recollective Fantasia

Verene has coined the term *recollective fantasia* to indicate the type of memory operative in Vico's science of origins. Recollective fantasia can be understood with reference to how the imaginative universal structures the memory of the first humans: "Recollective *fantasia* contains in itself elements that reflect in a one-to-one fashion the elements in the memory structure of original or mythic *fantasia*. It is the result of basing reflective thought on the image, rather than beginning with some notion of the concept and then working toward its concreteness."[20]

As the form of the *New Science*, recollective fantasia, then, refers to MEMORIA as functioning on a self-conscious level, as opposed to the nonreflexive activity of threefold memory in forming the humanness of the first humans. In addition, Vico's new science employs recollection and the maker's imagination based on the priority of the image, in contrast to reflection and logical implication, which are based on the priority of the concept.[21]

When the concept is given primary status in human cognition, the status of sense is downgraded, along with memory and imagination as an extension of sense. A rational metaphysics, as discussed earlier, "teaches that man becomes all things by understanding them" (405). And when man understands, "he extends his mind and takes in the things" (405).

Stephen Daniel notes that as a *self-conscious* activity (as a *science* that is reflexively aware of its *methodology*), "such an extension means going beyond the sensible, the figural, the communally experienced to that which does not fall under the senses. Such a move to the intelligible has to blind itself to the sensible basis of meaning."[22] A reflexive rational metaphysics adopts a certain mode of discourse and discovery "made possible by and generated through the emergence of reason and of abstracting, discursive ways of thinking . . . which loses touch with the perceptual immediacy of mythic invention."[23]

This privileging of the intelligible means that sense-bound phenomena are downgraded to the level of appearance, in contrast to the reality of the intelligible. This mode of thinking "shuts down" imagination and memory, "numbing" it through constricting threefold memory to the single dimension of the witnessing mode of consciousness (coscienza).

As Verene notes, under this view "the calling up of something in memory is not a form of knowledge but remains a psychological process unless connected with some fact or cognition."[24] Myth or fable, which function as structures of imagination and memory, then function as "opposites for truth, or synonyms for error."[25] In operating thus, discursive thinking *methodologically* cuts itself off from the *sensus communis*, the basis for human thinking in the sensible topics that structured the genesis of humanity. A new science that would recall these origins therefore requires something different from the methodology of critical or conceptual analysis.[26]

The problem Vico's new science faces is one of rebeginning thought in an age of abstract reflection; it must revive fantasia as a mode of discourse and discovery. It must initiate a reflexive use of the maker's imagination as a methodological imperative.[27] As the threefold memory functioned "collectively" to form the flux of sense into imaginative universals, so fantasia must function "recollectively" to order the archai of humanity in achieving scienza, maker's knowledge. The form of this memory is what Verene has termed the *recollective imaginative universal*.[28]

The archaic imaginative universals served to provide topoi that stabilized the sensory flux, providing orientation and meaning. Similarly, recollective imaginative universals provide topoi that orient us in the flux of human making, which are made up of such varied cose as "giants, sacrifices, poetic logic, monsters, metamorphoses, money, rhythm, song, children, poetic economy, Roman assemblies, the true Homer, heroic aristocracies, natural law, duels, Jean Bodin, legal metaphysics, barbaric history . . . the scenery of the human world."[29]

In recalling or re-collecting the original collections of humanity, the new science thus requires a master topos to structure the recollection, just as the master image of Jove initiated the formation of humanity in the first humans. The recollective master image in the new science is the *storia ideale eterna*, the ideal eternal history, and its function illustrates further the parallel functioning of collective and recollective fantasia.

The Common Nature of the Nations

The third edition of the *New Science*, which appeared in July 1744, six months after Vico's death, had as its title *Principi di scienza nuova di Giambattista Vico d'intorno alla comune nature della nazioni* (Principles of a new science of Giambattista Vico concerning the common nature of the nations).[30] Consider the phrase "common nature of the nations." Recall with Fisch that "the controlling methodological postulate of Vico's new science is that doctrines or theories must begin where the matters they treat begin," which means that "genesis, or becoming, is of the essence of that which the new science treats."[31] Given this, Fisch notes, we would expect "the common nature of the nations" to "involve an ontogenetic pattern exhibited by each nation in its origin, development, maturity, decline, and fall."[32]

A "nation" for Vico is a *nascimento*, a being born, or a birth. The peoples of a nation, then, have a shared origin in common, as well as a shared network of cose, or human things.[33] The first humans began to be truly human when they created these cose in the midst of the sensory flux. In so doing they created a *common sense*. Vico notes that "common sense is judgement without reflection, shared by an entire class, an entire people, an entire nation, or the entire human race" (142).[34] Thus, "there must in the nature of human things be a mental language common to all nations, which uniformly grasps the substance of things feasible in human social life and expresses it with as many diverse modifications as these same things may have diverse aspects" (161).

At their birth, for example, all *nazioni* had their moment of thunder, their Jove, which is the *cosa* of religion. The nature of that human thing is therefore nothing but its "being born [*nascimento*] at certain times and in certain guises" (147). The "certain time" a religion was born was when the sky thundered; the "certain guise," the condition of nefarious promiscuity in the flux. What was born was an archaic topos which then engendered two more cose, those of marriage and burial—and these three topoi became primary agents in the establishment of humanity.[35]

Recollective fantasia structures these particulars into the master image of the ideal eternal history (as Jove was structured through threefold memory into the master image of the human world). Recollective simple memory "fixes" the flux of cose—of one damn thing after another—into philological certains. It engenders a "philological sensibility" that enables us to identify "certain aspects, words, events, happenings" in the life of a past nation that allow us to return to it and understand it.[36] This is historical memory as commonly understood; being able to find "in artifacts and documents that exist in the present what is not present, what is not here and now."[37] We remember the cose, the human things.

Fantasia takes these remembered cose and extends and compounds them into a human whole: "la fantasia . . . altro none è che memoria o diltata o composta" (211). A specific philological understanding is in this way compounded into a *storia* with which we can identify, a living human whole. [38] The life of past ages is imaginatively reconstructed (in this powerful sense of imagination) in a way that allows us to reexperience these past forms of life (in the same way the first men could reexperience Jove). Recollective ingegno, then, "frames" the felt whole, allowing us to sense the pattern of interconnections that constitute its larger meaning. This process of framing the whole gives us a philosophical sense of history, a sense that history has a meaning we can descry. [39]

It is fantasia that holds the philology of simple memory and the philosophy of ingegno together, enabling us to recollect the particulars as a felt human whole. The power of the maker's imagination to think these particulars in universal form, then, "requires a master image of the human world in terms of which we can have access both to it as a whole and to any one of its concrete particulars." [40] This master image is the ideal eternal history, "the first name of recollective consciousness," which is providence. [41] It appears suddenly, like the thunder, providing instant orientation in the flux of human possibility. We do not grasp it discursively but can perceive it only in an act of imaginative reconstruction. [42]

Reflective thinking, Vico tells us, when faced with the particulars of the human world, seems driven into a dilemma, finding in history either the deaf necessity (*sorda necessità*) of the Stoics or the blind chance (*cieco caso*) of the Epicureans. The metaphysics of the concept is unable to form the experience of history into a human whole; it can only, as Verene so nicely puts it, "strike conceptual poses" in the face of the human event. [43] Calm and abstractive, the conceptual approach is unable to feel the terror and tragedy in history that can give rise to the image of providence. It cannot feel the thunder that will generate the whole.

The terror and the tragedy of history is found in the pattern that is suddenly descried: "Men first feel necessity, then look for utility, next attend to comfort, still later amuse themselves with pleasure, thence grow dissolute in luxury, and finally go mad and waste their substance" (241). The metaphysician of the concept cannot feel the fear the image engenders and banishes it through the strategies of an Epicurus or a Descartes. But the cycle of a nation, the *corso* that necessarily revolves through the stages of birth, maturity, and decline, begins in necessity and ends in madness. [44] To feel this is to have a fundamental perception of the strangeness and unfamiliarity of which we are a part; a strangeness and unfamiliarity we are then able to connect with and in which we can find a meaning.

As "feeling things" rather than "thinking things," we find ourselves intimate with the process of the ideal eternal history. We see it in our own lives, as well as in the lives of others. We can see that "out of the passions of men, each bent on his private advantage, for the sake of which they would live like wild beasts in the wilderness," divine providence "has made the civil institutions [*ordine civile*] by which they may live in human society" (133). We feel the thunder of history and shake. We have, perhaps for the first time, a truly human thought.

In considering the circle of history, Vico notes that "since these things have been established by divine providence, the course of the institutions of the nations had to be, must now be, and will have to be such as our Science demonstrates" (348). In order for the philological certainties that we witness through simple recollective memory to attain decisive proof for us, we must act as makers and take up our position as a created gods: "Indeed, we make bold to affirm that he who meditates this Science narrates to himself this history so far as he himself makes it for himself by that proof 'it had, has, and will have to be'" (349).

And it is in this making that man properly imitates God: "And this very fact is an argument, O reader, that these proofs are of a kind divine and should give thee a divine pleasure, since in God knowledge and creation are one and the same thing" (349). Such a pleasure is consonant with the melancholy that also results from the perception we gain of the whole , for the whole is a place of thundering terror. We feel pleasure and melancholy, for Vico's science is a knowledge of things human as well as divine.

It should by now be clear that when Vico speaks of axioms, corollaries, and the geometric method, he is not intending his (insightful) readers to expect a deductive system. The philosophy of the maker's imagination has more to offer us than this, if we are prepared to unthink the obvious.

And we are now in a position to appreciate Ernst Cassirer's comment that in Vico, "for the first time logic dared to break through the circle of mathematics and natural science, and dared instead to constitute itself as the logic of . . . language, poetry, and history."[45] Vico's logos is one unfamiliar to us, although it should also seem hauntingly familiar through our archaic roots when we dream or truly and creatively imagine.

How are we to understand the method of such a logos of language, poetry, and history? What are the governing roots of this system of thought? How can we understand what Vico means by an axiom in terms of his philosophy of the maker's imagination? If we do not expect the unexpected, we will never find out.

When Isaiah Berlin speaks of Vico's thought as "an ill-assorted mass of ideas . . . all jostling each other in the chaos of his . . . badly ordered and overburdened mind," it becomes clear how Berlin (and thinkers like him) have unaccountably missed the true intent of Vico's attempt to found a philosophy upon the priority of the image over the concept.[46] The unfamiliar passes by them, and they do not fully recognize it.

It passes them by because Vico's thought seems to them a jumble of discordant elements that have no inner coherence. They see, not the other, but only their own reflections, clear and distinct, in the mirror of their own thought and times. In the words of Heraclitus, "They do not understand how being at variance it agrees with itself: there is a back-stretched connectedness, as in the bow and the lyre" (fr. 51).

5 The Roots of Rhetoric

Vico was, of course, a professor of rhetoric, and even a cursory reading of his *Institutiones oratoriae* makes one aware of his detailed knowledge—down to the minutiae of the topical method—of the conventional rhetoric of his day. Yet as I stated in Chapter 1 with respect to Renaissance humanism, although Vico began with the conventional rhetoric of his time, he did not end up there.

Verene notes that Vico did not simply equate philosophy with rhetoric. The *Scienza nuova* is not Cicero's rhetoric in modern dress. Instead, "Vico rejoins philosophy with its roots in ancient poetic and rhetoric and with its Renaissance ties to these humanist activities, but he does so in order to accomplish a philosophic vision of truth."[1] It is a new way of thinking, a new method, embodied in the new book of wisdom that is the *Scienza nuova*.

Vico's new method steered a middle way through the quarrel between the ancients and the moderns that was current in his day. For Vico was not alone in inheriting the Renaissance and confronting modernity; this confrontation in many ways defined the intellectual atmosphere of his time. The debate between the partisans of synthetic (Euclidian) geometry and those of the new analytical geometry, which involved Vico's friend Paolo Mattia Doria, is one instance of this—as is the French *querelle* of letters in the works of Bernard le Bovier de Fontenelle and Charles Perrault.[2] Yet Vico did not end up as a partisan for the ancients or the moderns; or rather, he descended through this debate to investigate the origins of the difference between the ancient and modern approaches to knowledge.[3] This descent gave him a position outside the quarrel from which to view its participants.

Methods of Study

We can find a starting point for Vico's descent in his *Study Methods*. In this oration he takes as his topic: "Which method of studies is finer and better, ours or the ancients'?" (*SM* 5/791). He then immediately adds, "Unless I am mistaken, this theme is new; but the knowledge of it is so important, that I am amazed it has not been treated yet" (*SM* 5/791). And in the conclusion of the oration he notes that "the fact that a theme is new is not automatically a recommendation; monstrous and ridiculous things may also be novelties. But to bring forward new things and to treat them in the right manner is unquestionably worthy of praise. Whether I did so, or not, I shall leave to the judgement of my listeners" (*SM* 79–80/853).[4]

Vico is here, as usual, concerned to achieve a descent to the *archai*—the governing roots of the phenomenon under consideration. He wishes to descend to the roots of the quarrel; not to subsume analysis under topics, or vice versa, but to achieve a heroic balance between the two, and thus achieve self-knowledge. Verene notes that for Vico, "the mind is at its zenith, like the heroic, when it can balance its opposites, each of which has its rightful claim. The heroic is never a choice of good against bad, of light over darkness, but rather a surmounting of the two in some way, never actually joining or synthesizing them."[5]

Vico gives us an early example of his new and developing method of studies in his oration concerning the ancient and modern method of studies.[6] His purpose is not just to play off the ancient against the modern but to point to a new approach in the face of the modern confrontation with the ancient, which had created a split between *pathos* and *logos*, feeling and reason, as epitomized in Cartesian method. A mere nostalgia for the ancients is seen to be as worthless as a mere contempt.[7]

Vico states in the *Study Methods* that "in Greece, a single philosopher synthesized in himself a whole university" (*SM* 74/849).[8] But in modern times "the arts and sciences, all of which in the past were embraced by philosophy and anointed by it with a unitary spirit, are, in our day, unnaturally separated and disjointed" (*SM* 76/851). Education becomes "so warped and perverted as a consequence, that, although [students] may become extremely learned in some respects, their culture on the whole (and the whole is really the flower of wisdom) is incoherent" (*SM* 77/851).

Vico returns to this topos in his address to the Academy of Oziosi, *The Academies and the Relation between Philosophy and Eloquence.* Here he contrasts the modern academy with the ideal of Socrates, who established an academy where "he, with eloquence, copiousness, and ornament, reasoned about all parts of human and divine knowing" (*AR* 86/938).

In such an environment pathos and logos were not split. Instead, heart and language were "reunited in their natural bond, which Socrates, full of philosophy in language and heart, had firmly brought together." But there was an inevitable decline from this archaic "place." Outside of it "a violent divorce existed: the sophists experienced a vain art of speaking and the philosophers a dry and unadorned manner of speaking" (*AR* 86/938).

When a return to the ancient balance through the (mere) cultivation of ancient thought (such as Averroës' commentaries on Aristotle) was attempted, a scholastic blindness developed. This revival of the ancients became "bereft of light, lacking in any softness or color, a cloying manner of reasoning, always in the same syllogistic form and quite spiritless gait, enumerating each order of discourse" (*AR* 87/939).

And the Cartesian philosophy that reacted against this scholasticism was really no better off, for it too ignored the balanced whole that is the flower of wisdom: "Placing the total force of its proofs in the geometric method, such a method is so subtle and drawn out that if by chance attention to one proposition is broken, it is completely lost to whoever is listening to comprehend anything of the whole of what is being said" (*AR* 87/939). Blind nostalgia and contemptuous innovation are alike insufficient to achieve a balance that addresses the whole.

What is needed, says Vico, is eloquence, which addresses the balanced whole in the tension of essential opposition. He cites Demosthenes as an example, whose archai are to be found in the Platonic academy founded by Socrates. "Demosthenes," he notes, "came forth from the Platonic academy where he had listened for a good eight years, and he came armed with his invincible enthymeme." Through the enthymeme Demosthenes became master, forming it "by means of a very well regulated excess, going outside his case into quite different things with which he tempered the lightning flashes of his arguments" (*AR* 87/939).

And the balancing in this way of the "quite different things" in the macrocosm is then balanced in the microcosm as well. Wit, or *ingenium,* which might be described as the power to think enthymemically, is instrumental in achieving an inner as well as an outer connection (the two are not strictly separable anyway).

Verene notes that the logical ground of the Vichian project is the human need for self-knowledge. Vico's philosophy in general is thus dominated by the quest for that knowledge.[9] In his first oration Vico states that "as a sphere rotates on its axis, so does my argument hinge on this: knowledge of oneself."[10]

Vico held to that orientation to the end of his work. The object of his new scienza was the knower himself, as he is integrated with the civil world, rather than a knowledge of God or nature.[11] And since the self is rooted in the world of civil things, one turns inward through turning outward. One does *not* state, as does Descartes, "I shall now close my eyes, I shall stop my ears, I shall call away all my senses, I shall efface even from my thoughts all the images of corporeal things, or at least (for that is hardly possible) I shall esteem them as vain and false; and thus holding converse with myself and considering my own nature, I shall try little by little to reach a better knowledge of . . . myself."[12] For Vico, one does not achieve self-knowledge in the transparencies of the *cogito* but in the opaque cose of the civil world.

How can we understand Vico's comments on the whole and on eloquence? What does he mean by enthymemic thinking, and how are we to understand its relation to the fragmentation of modern thought? What is the relation of enthymemic thinking as Vico came to understand it to the rhetorical tradition in which he grew up? And how did he descend through the tradition of commonplace to a fresh vision of Aristotelian rhetoric—then descend again through that to the roots of concept and of imagination in the thinking of the first humans? The first step in answering these questions is to understand certain key elements of the commonplace tradition.

The Commonplace Tradition

The use of topoi, loci, or commonplaces pervaded Renaissance pedagogy to an extent that is hard for us to imagine, so different are modern habits of thought and learning. As Joan Marie Lechner notes, once a modern reader becomes "familiar with the rhetorical principles which were imbibed by every Renaissance schoolboy, and their relation to the commonplaces, he will find on every page examples of the directing influences of these exercises."[13]

Lechner's statement holds true of Vico as well. Vico's new science was born in just this milieu; it was what he descended through in achieving his new science, giving it a characteristic guise discernible to anyone familiar with the habits of topical thinking that influenced its nature or birth.[14]

Classical Roots

Topoi have been referred to in two dominant ways in the commonplace tradition: either as a locale in mental or imaginative space that "contains" arguments or as a speech-within-a-speech that amplifies the subject under consideration. The two usages supplemented each other and often seem interchangeable. As we shall see, the notion of the loci is a very fluid one indeed.[15]

Aristotle is generally saddled by tradition with the notion of the topos as a locale or container in the mind, although as I will show, he perhaps had a more dynamic notion of the places than the tradition allowed. *Topos*, of course, literally means "place," as in a region or a physical position. It becomes, metaphorically, that locale or space where the speaker, in the practice of his of her art, can look for lines of inquiry or available means of persuasion.[16] As George A. Kennedy notes, "Although the word accords with Aristotle's fondness for visual imagery, he did not originate its use in the sense of 'topic.' Isocrates, early in the fourth century, had so used it, and probably others before him."[17] And the fact that Aristotle nowhere in the *Topics* or the *Rhetoric* defines *topos* would seem to mean that he assumed the word would be understood, which supports the contention that he inherited this notion. Taking up the topical rubric, Aristotle gave it his own interpretation (while attempting to mediate, as was his wont, everyday knowledge).[18]

William J. Grimaldi states that the idea of topics was operative before Aristotle and that it appears that "collections of *topoi* were made which were concerned for the most part with material and lines of argument specific to a definite, limited problem or case."[19] These would then be used when similar cases arose. Aristotle's contribution, according to Grimaldi, was to "derive and describe the method at work, and he may have kept the name *topoi* for the method since it describes the process: these are the places from which originate both the material and the formal elements in all dialectical and rhetorical discussion."[20]

The commonplace tradition took from Aristotle the division into general and specific topics. Topics were either common, embodying universal arguments used in all the sciences, or specific, relating to a particular subject, like physics. Commonplaces were also divided into four subsets: possible or impossible, greater or less, past or future, and magnified or minimized. Subsequent treatments of the places accepted these divisions as basic and generally retained the Aristotelian essentials.[21]

Cicero in particular emphasized the concept of the topos as a mental locale which served as a container for arguments. He states: "It is easy to find things that are hidden if the hiding place is pointed out and marked; similarly if we wish to track down some argument we ought to know the places or topics: for that is the name given by Aristotle to the 'regions,' as it were, from which arguments are drawn. Accordingly, we may define a topic as the region of an argument."[22]

Alongside the rubrics of the locale or container were those of the little oration, or speech-within-a-speech. Apthonius, a contemporary of Aristotle's, thought of the places in this way. These little orations then served as places within the speech that amplified or minimized its subject.[23] As Lechner notes, this approach takes one of Aristotle's four divisions—magnification and minimization—and makes it primary.[24] In the tradition the same loci were sometimes thought of as places from which to draw forth arguments, as well as little orations that amplified, and thus embellished, the larger speech. She notes that the little orations were considered as commonplaces because "they provided ready-made 'arguments' which in some way magnified (or minimized) a subject."[25] As well, they were thought of spatially, as ornaments or containers of arguments located within the space of the larger speech.

The two primary spatial metaphors were a location for arguments in some sort of spatial field and a container for arguments. Lechner notes that the topical tradition, consciously or unconsciously, embraced the idea of "ideological space," which the idea of the places as such implies. This idea is not developed in a self-consciously analytical sense, by an examination of its psychological bases, but through the allowing of "the original metaphor embedded in the concept to spawn a seemingly unlimited number of related or subsidiary metaphors."[26]

According to Lechner, the areas in which the loci were metaphorically positioned included forests, gardens, military camps, or plains of battle, which varied according to the imagination of the speaker. She writes that "the process of invention was to familiarize the orator with the 'place where' he could find the arguments and recognize them instantly."[27] The activity of invention was then pictured in images commensurate with the primary spatial metaphors. One could either hunt for an argument, seeking to locate and identify it (which implies a locale or region in which to search), assemble arguments (which implies a construction in space), or store the arguments or hide them away and then take them back out again (which implies a containing space for the arguments).

All these metaphors involve what Lechner terms the "spatial coefficient," which increased enormously in Roman rhetoric, being particularly emphasized by Cicero and Quintillian. And this emphasis had a profound influence on Renaissance concepts of knowledge, as intellectual activity and communication were dominated by a reduction to a kind of local motion.[28] The practical consequence was that "this spatializing of knowledge helped give currency to the Renaissance idea that universal knowledge could be contained within the pages of the commonplace books. The dialectical and rhetorical places, with their metaphorical imagery, stored indiscriminately but in great mass within these books, were considered the *loci* of the entire 'circle' of the arts and sciences."[29] These were the rubrics of the commonplaces in the classical world: what about their uses? What was the praxis of the commonplaces?

The use of the "places" seems to arise with the Sophists in the second half of the fifth century BCE in Greece. It arose first in the context of what is sometimes called dialectic, which involved the realization that one could argue both for and against any position, owing to the diploid character of reality.[30] Perhaps the most famous statement of this position is the so-called *dissoi logoi* fragment of Protagoras found in Diogenes Laertius. According to Diogenes, Protagoras said that "there are two *logoi* in opposition to each other about every thing."[31]

The heart of this claim is not that an eristic debate can be generated on any subject matter (although that is a consequence of the more fundamental claim that there are two logoi in opposition to each other about everything). Rather, reality is such that we can find two opposing accounts in any experience; as Mario Untersteiner puts it, there are "two *logoi* which invest all experience."[32] Rhetoric is concerned with reality and the account we give of it. Here we see an early awareness of the inseparability of *verba* and *res*, word and thing, which was to become so evident in Cicero.[33]

Rhetoric had for these thinkers what we might call an epistemological and ontological dimension. As Grimaldi puts it, the primary concern of thinkers like Isocrates and Aristotle was "the ability of the mind to know and apprehend meaning in the world of reality and to interpret this knowledge to others."[34] This means that when a human being finds himself needing to make a judgment in the world of reality, "he puts before himself or others those reasons which not only represent the real facts or real situation insofar as he can apprehend them, but which are also the more convincing to himself or to his auditors. When we say 'more convincing' . . . we are simply accepting the inescapable fact that in all areas of human living there are large complexes of pre-existing convictions and assumptions within which we must attempt to speak to the other."[35] These "complexes" are the commonplaces; the human realities which compose the sensus communis.

Cicero reflects this concern in his distinction between memoria concerning res and memoria concerning verba.[36] Defining the five parts of rhetoric, he writes: "Invention is the excogitation of true things [res], or things similar enough to truth to render one's cause plausible; disposition is the arrangement in order of the things discovered; elocution is the accommodation of suitable words to the invented [things]; memory is the firm perception in the soul of things and words; pronunciation is the moderating of the voice and body to suit the dignity of the things and words."[37]

As Frances Yates notes, the aim of the rhetorician is to cultivate memoria in such a way that one firmly grasps both things and words.[38] When an orator is being persuasive and eloquent, then, his words should be organically related to the realities of the situation he is addressing. Someone is precisely *not* being rhetorical *enough* when he panders to the emotions of his audience by painting a false picture of their situation. He is then being a bad (that is, unskilled or nonvirtuous) rhetorician. It was Cicero's insistence on practicing a skillful rhetoric that put his head on a pike.

The practice of finding the two logoi, then, whatever its ontological grounding, reflected the development of the logical side of topics. And so, out of this practice arose the notion of invention: discovering lines of argument or ways of approach to the *pragma*, the matter in question.

The practical orientation of sophistic education accentuated this development. The Sophists, after all, were educating young men for the political life of the city-states, which was dominated by public speaking in the assemblies and courts. Under the sophistic model of education, a master prepared a model speech on standard poetic, political, or moral themes that was then copied down and memorized for delivery by the pupil.

As Lechner notes, an effective speech had to have more than form: it needed a real content to expand the subject under consideration. There was a practical need for the student to invent or discover the two opposed ways to argue the theme, as well as a way to make it relevant to the audience. In this manner the branch of rhetoric devoted to invention (or discovery) arose.[39]

This attention to invention, which sought to discover two opposing logoi in every experience, gave rise to an awareness of certain set patterns of relevant considerations that could be applied to set occasions for speech. Lechner states that in this way "invention gave rise to the commonplaces or topics which enabled one to analyze everything and anything because they were of universal concern and treated of such concepts as justice and injustice, nature and convention, and the like. These were the famous commonplaces."[40]

Here we again see that the early use of commonplaces involved "natural" pairings, the idea being that one could find in any subject at issue two lines of argument to and from the issue (the pairing of *nomos* and *phusis*, law and nature, represents a classic example of this). The concern was formal in both a stylistic and a logical sense, although the logical side of the commonplaces did not receive their due until Aristotle. To bring out both sides of the question in the appropriate manner, to ring the changes on the commonplaces, became a mark of eloquence and thoroughness in an implicitly logical sense.

The commonplaces have also always been associated with the adornment and enrichment of language.[41] Aristotle devoted the third book of the *Rhetoric* to what he called *lexis*, arrangement or style, and he seemed to think it an essential aspect of the subject. The Roman orators placed an even greater emphasis on adornment (although not greater, one would think, than Isocrates). Cicero thought that a speech was rendered distinguished or brilliant when commonplaces were introduced.[42] He wrote that "all the ornaments of style, which lend charm and dignity, are lavished on common topics, as well as everything which in the invention of matter or thought contributes to weight and grandeur."[43] And Quintillian added that these ornaments should not be something artificially memorized and injected into the speech but that instead "the sentiments should spring from the context."[44]

Isocrates injected another feature into the commonplace tradition which was to become both characteristic and all-embracing: that of its involvement with *prudentia*. For Isocrates, practical concerns of conduct "were intimately joined with rhetorical invention and judgment."[45] He stated that these concerns "characterize men who ignore our practical needs and delight in the mental juggling of the ancient sophists as 'students of philosophy,' but refuse this name to those who pursue and practice those studies which will enable us to govern wisely both our own households and the commonwealth."[46]

Isocrates thus scorned the notion, as George Norlin puts it, that "the art of oratory is easily acquired by learning, largely from example, a number of elements or commonplaces which may be put together, like the letters of the alphabet, into speeches appropriate and effective for any occasion; whereas in fact, oratory is not something which may be learned by rote from a master, but is a creative art which requires of the student a vigorous and imaginative mind."[47]

So, as Lechner notes, the stylistic attention given to the common-places in speeches was for Isocrates and his followers "but the outward manifestation of the deference commanded by their implicitly moral content."[48] As used in a humanistic education, the commonplaces should address the actualities and probabilities of one's civic and social life. Isocrates states that "since it is not in the nature of man to attain a science by the possession of which we can know positively what we should do or what we should say, in the next resort I hold that man to be wise who is able by his powers of conjecture to arrive generally at the best course, and I hold that man to be a philosopher who occupies himself with studies from which he will most quickly gain that kind of insight."[49]

Eloquence, then, along with its logical concomitants, was essentially allied with prudential considerations (which are not to be thought of as having as narrow an extension as pragmatic ones). According to Lechner, because the topics of rhetoric "dealt with key ideas, and hence with those likely to be adaptable and 'common' to every human situation, they tended to gravitate toward themes of virtue and vice."[50] Cicero would take up these notions in a way that profoundly affected the Renaissance. For the Roman orators seemed to gravitate naturally toward such concerns.

It is itself another commonplace that the classical milieu in which the praxis of the commonplaces developed was overwhelmingly oral. The political and cultural life of the Greek city-states revolved around public debate in the assemblies and law courts, and political power was often a function of proficiency in this oral praxis. Kennedy notes that decisions on public policy "were made in regularly held assemblies composed of adult male citizens; and as in New England town meetings, anyone who wished could speak. Not surprisingly, however, the leadership role in debate was played by a small number of ambitious individuals called *rhetores*, who sought to channel the course of events in a direction which they thought was best for the city or for themselves."[51]

And there were no professional lawyers. This meant that "if people wished to seek redress in the courts for some wrong done them—and the Greeks were very fond of going to law—or if people were summoned to court as defendants, they were expected to speak on their own behalf."[52]

If one then adds to the political and legal dimensions the primacy of theater, poetry, public addresses on state occasions, and the like, it is not surprising that the classical rhetorical tradition emphasized the *technē*, the art or skill of oral discourse. Grimaldi writes that Aristotle's work on rhetoric reflects this oral emphasis, echoing the original concerns of the speaker and giving them new depth. So for Aristotle, "the rhetorical *techne* includes within its ambience any subject open to discussion . . . it attends to all the aspects of that subject which admit of verbal presentation and which are necessary to make the subject understandable and acceptable to an other."[53]

The key elements of the classical tradition that I wish to emphasize can be summarized as follows:

- the spatial rubrics and coefficient
- the ontological dimension (res and verba)
- eloquence and its logical concomitants
- prudentia and its stylistic concomitants
- the emphasis on oral performance.

The Renaissance would appropriate all these aspects of the topical tradition, giving them its own peculiar emphases.

Renaissance Shoots

From the age of Quintillian to that of Augustine—the so-called Second Sophistic—pedagogy followed a pattern laid down by the earlier rhetoricians, who had stressed oral speech (in the assembly and the courts), but in practice it became a preparation for written amplification.[54] Throughout the Second Sophistic and into the medieval period, a shrinking "civil space" and a corresponding abandonment of the courtroom and political assemblies by the orator led rhetoric to become conventional. As Lechner characterized it, "Arrangement was supplanted by pattern, memory became verbal, style and delivery were now the main reliance, and they were elaborated into an intensely technical system."[55] Oral performance had declined into textual display.

In this way the commonplace method spread out from the oral provinces of teaching and preaching into "all of the *ars dictaminis*, historical and religious biography, philosophical and theological argument, ecclesiastical and legal controversies."[56] *Commonplaces* came to mean collections of proverbs and maxims for amplifying written texts and were no longer the seats of arguments as in the works of "Aristotle," Cicero, and Quintillian.[57]

By the twelfth century, in works such as John of Salisbury's *Metalogicon*, "the consignment of rhetoric to the formation of adorning and dilating took from it something of its former vitality in the intellectual processes of composition."[58] Logic became the discipline of the serious thinker, which led invention to become the province of logic in the trivium.[59]

In consequence, logic (thought of as dialectic) and rhetoric became widely separated. This was contrary to the spirit of classical rhetoric, which had urged a rapprochement between the two. The attitude that separated the two hearkened back to Zeno, who, Cicero reports, "as the founder of the Stoic school, used to give an object lesson of the difference between the two arts; clenching his fist, he said logic was like that; relaxing and extending his hand, he said eloquence was like the open palm."[60] Cicero himself advocated that "the man of perfect eloquence" not only speak well but "acquire that neighboring borderland science of logic"; for both are concerned with discourse, which is the province of the eloquent man.[61] Rhetoric is thus broader than logic and contains it.[62]

Certain thinkers in the Renaissance revived this pagan understanding, and thus the trend toward the separation of logic and rhetoric was counterbalanced by a tendency to find dialectic and rhetoric reciprocally related in oratory.[63] According to Lechner, "proof of this is found in the various treatises on the tropes and figures of style, in which, even though the emphasis is overwhelmingly on . . . rhetorical places, the figures of thought are also prominent. These figures of thought include what would properly be called dialectical places—*sententiae*, *chria*, proverb, definition, etymology and division."[64] But this was only a "rear-guard action" which would fight its last battles, with the Cartesians, in Vico's own day.

In this fashion the logical concern for argument (which at this time equalled the syllogistic) became fused with more rhetorical concerns in the humanist revival. Phillipp Melanchthon wrote in his *Elementorum rhetorice*

(1572) that "the commonplace contains the major premise of the syllogism. . . . The places are fonts of ornaments and regions of arguments."[65]

Because of this, invention became concerned with finding the middle term of the syllogism. Valerius discusses in his *Philosophia vetus et nova* (1678) the central necessity of "finding" the middle in order to prove the subject. To do this the commonplaces are brought in, which is why rhetoricians "invent so many commonplaces."[66] These middle terms, or loci, are then thought to "walk around the whole body of the subject," helping to define it.[67]

The Isocratean emphasis on style yoked inseparably with a prudential concern was also revived by Renaissance thinkers. During medieval times the commonplaces had been exploited for theological purposes, which had essentially destroyed their moral relevance; but with the revival of pagan ideals, the pagan virtues again became a norm for human conduct, and the commonplaces once again implicated moral conduct.[68]

Rhetoric underlay instruction in all fields, which meant that training in the use of topics was omnipresent as well. Since the loci were "necessarily bound up with moral sentences, aphorisms, and proverbial sayings . . . the long tedious hours spent by the students in memorizing, paraphrasing, and expanding axioms of virtue would so color their way of thinking that everything and everybody tended to be viewed through one or the other set of glasses as clothed in the whiteness of virtue or the blackness of vice."[69] A writer like Shakespeare, for example, seemed incapable by his training "of writing about anything outside a virtue-vice—that is, an intensely personal and human—framework."[70]

Morality and eloquence combined in the sixteenth and seventeenth centuries in an aphoristic style of writing which was to culminate in works as diverse as Francis Bacon's *Novum organon* and Baltasar Gracián's *Oráculo manual y arte de prudencia*. The common factor in writings like these was the concentration of meaning in a witty (that is, not obvious) manner. Commenting on this style of writing, Christopher Maurer notes that such stylistic habits are easy to recognize: they include "antithesis and paradox; the constant use of ellipses; the concentration of meaning brought about by punning and other sorts of wordplay; the lack of connective tissue between one sentence—one point—and another (notice that there is often an abrupt transition between aphorism and commentary, and that the commentaries themselves often seem disjointed and fragmentary)."[71]

The aphoristic style, then, became closely associated with the idea of the commonplace book, which in its turn became closely associated with the idea of artificial memory.

The idea of the commonplace book goes back to Aristotle, who advocated that "we should select also from the written handbooks of argument, and should draw up sketch lists of some of each kind of subject, putting them in separate lists, as 'On good,' or 'On Life'—and 'On Good' should deal with all good, beginning with what good is. In the margin, too, one should indicate also the opinion of individuals, for example, 'Empedocles said that the elements were four': for anyone might assent to the saying of some generally accepted authority."[72]

Renaissance instruction was dominated by the assemblage of these books. Pupils, for example, kept such books from their earliest schooling as a regular adjunct to *all* their areas of study.[73] And the actual practice of assembling the commonplace book stayed amazingly close to Aristotle's original prescription, although in its final progression into the artificial memory systems it illustrated an amazing development. We can hardly imagine two things more different than a simple commonplace book and the memory theater of Camillo, but, as we shall see in Chapter 8, they share a common root.

Lechner notes that "the use of the commonplace collections as an aid to memory is perhaps one of the key motives for the popularity and long endurance of such a method."[74] The practice of keeping such books, then, was aimed at developing ingenium, as well as from a desire for a general knowledge of the arts and sciences.[75] Bacon wrote, for example, that although some people thought that keeping commonplace books was detrimental to learning, "nevertheless, as it is but a counterfeit thing in knowledge to be forward and pregnant, except a man be also deep and full, I hold diligence and labor in the entry of common places to be a matter of great use and support . . . as that which supplies matter to invention, and contracts the sight of judgement to a point."[76]

In the Renaissance the commonplace books were often thought of as artificial memories, which would supplement the natural one; a sort of organon to extend the powers of memory. The idea of the artificial memory is thus intimately bound up with topical method and was indeed often referred to as "topical memory," the strength of which was determined by both nature and art.[77]

The art of memory is traced back by Cicero to the famous story of Simonides and the banquet.[78] After Simonides had left a party, the story goes, the roof collapsed, killing all within. Simonides was able to remember the identity of the guests by recalling the *place* at which each sat, visualizing their locations *spatially* in his imagination. The moral of the story, according to Cicero, is that Simonides realized that "persons desiring to train this faculty [of memory] must select places and form mental images of the things [rei] they wish to remember and store those images in the places, so that the order of the places will preserve the order of things, and the images of the things will denote the things themselves, and we shall employ the places and images respectively as a wax-writing tablet and the letters written in it."[79]

The key notion here is the association of places and images in memory. The loci frame an imaginative space in which the images are placed in a definite order. The most common framework was an architectural space.[80] Yates writes that "we have to think of the ancient orator as moving in imagination through his memory building whilst he is making his speech, drawing from the memorized places the images he has placed on them."[81]

The images in "memory space" are what Aristotle called archai, or governing roots. He states in *De memoria* that in order to recollect something "one must get hold of a governing root."[82] He then adds that "this is why some in recollecting something seem to proceed from places. The reason is that they pass swiftly from one point to the next, as from milk to white, from white to mist, and thence to moist, from which one recollects Autumn, if this is the season one is trying to recollect."[83]

Following the discussion of how to use the places as governing roots of recollection, Aristotle seems to hint at the notion of the artificial memory. He writes that in recollection "custom now assumes the role of nature . . . for as in nature one thing follows another, so also in the actualization—and here frequency makes it a nature."[84] Aristotle thus seems to indicate two kinds of memory, one a function of nature and the other function of custom (and thus a made, or artificial, memory).

The classic and explicit distinction between natural and artificial memory is found in *Ad Herrenium*, composed by an unknown teacher of rhetoric in Rome around 86–82 BCE.[85] In it, the author writes that "there are, then, two kinds of memory: one natural, and the other a product of art. The natural memory is that memory which is embedded in our minds, born simultaneously with thought. The artificial memory is that memory which is strengthened by a kind of training and a system of discipline."[86]

The idea of the artificial memory, like the places and the commonplace books themselves, was also intertwined with moral and prudential concerns. Yates cites Cicero as the explicit source of this linkage (although, as we have seen, it is a characteristically Isocratean notion). Cicero stated that "wisdom is the knowledge of what is good, what is bad, and what is neither good nor bad. Its parts are memory [*memoria*], intelligence [*intelligentia*], and foresight [*providentia*]."[87] Memory is a part of wisdom.

From medieval times on into the Renaissance this definition of *prudentia*, which lists memoria as one of its parts, became joined with the idea of the artificial memory. It was argued by Saint Thomas, for example, that if memory is part of prudence it is ethically wise to cultivate the artificial as well as the natural memory. This notion itself became another Renaissance commonplace.[88]

The commonplace books had long included verbal descriptions of the imaginary places of memory. The memory spaces within which the images were placed included forests, gardens, mirrors, or theaters populated by the ancients.[89] And Lechner notes that "Bacon, Harvey, and Talon all refer to the logical topics . . . as the soul, or as the nerves and sinew giving support and life to the body."[90] It was only natural, with all the emphasis on imaginative imagery, that the next step would be to import actual images into the commonplace books (which were thought of as artificial memory systems). This was something new, rather than a continuation of the style of Lull, who in his medieval system of memory had employed images as a mnemonic symbolic logic.[91] For these "emblem books," as they came to be called, relied upon a sophisticated and self-conscious awareness of the *interaction* between image and text.

Charles Mosley notes that the medieval and Renaissance grammarians recognized the problematic nature of language and its difficulties in communicating what it wants to. The grammarians thought that these difficulties might be addressed through carefully constructed images built into the text. In this way the imagination could act as a "control" on the merely verbal.[92] To achieve this, Mosley writes, the new commonplace books employed emblems as an adjunct to the text "which go well beyond mere decorations, for by inserting them and their symbolism the reading of the text is modified. The combination indicates an awareness of the ambiguity of language and that extraction of the meaning of the book is a complex, arduous and not obvious business."[93]

Such emblems were meant to be "ingenious," in the sense that one would need to employ the faculty of ingenium, or wit, to see the point of the symbolism. And as we might expect, as a part of the topical tradition, the attention to style carried with it a concern for prudence and morality. The emblem's form found its ultimate justification in its moral concern: "Properly used by a reader it offers counsel about action and the pursuit of . . . wisdom in the real world. . . . The symbolical design and its verbal accompaniments, of equal importance, are to teach a moral truth so that memory will grasp it not as a mere formula but . . . as an experience which will be a guide to understanding and conduct."[94]

These emblems were also seen as metaphors that would tell a story to those with the ingenium necessary to make the proper connections. And here again we note the emphasis on an organic connection with "real things" (here too res and verba combine). Mosley writes that "complex and extended metaphor is thought of as 'reversible': that is, the issue under discussion is conceived in the mind with the help of metaphor, but the validity of the metaphor is then tested by the experience of the real thing to which it refers."[95]

But the story the emblem qua metaphor tells is no simple one, offering a one-to-one mapping between tale and reality. It was a commonplace of the time, Mosley notes, that both poetry and painting signify in a nonliteral manner. This was especially true of the visual symbol, which meant that "the primacy of the functional purpose of metaphor and symbol allows verisimilitude to be ignored when it would clash with symbolic meaning."[96] The emblem was essentially a fable in brief. Mosley points out that "the coherence of the metaphorics of a work becomes more important than any surface naturalism."[97] And this was all an artful and self-conscious procedure, grounded in the principles of those like Marsilio Ficino, who thought that the arts communicate by fable and metaphor those things that cannot adequately be communicated in any other way.[98]

The emblem book thus compresses meaning in the same way a maxim does, offering fables in brief, which are to be unpacked by ingenium—but with the added complexity of visual-verbal interaction. Mosley gives an excellent summary of the complexity and elegance of the emblem book which I quote here in full:

> In an important way, therefore, the emblem's compound form points to the serious philosophic business of *how* the pursuit of knowledge may be conducted, and forces the alert reader to consider how his mind reads and understands. These points are highlighted by the way the verses can be presented. First, the signification of a picture can be explained directly: but the reader may see things other than he is being told. Or a dialogue between the voice of the verses and the figure in the picture can leave the reader as a spectator who has to evaluate each voice as well as the picture. Thirdly, a narrator's voice can simply address the picture and ignore the reader; again, the reader is as interested in what the narrator sees or does not see as well as what he does. Yet again, where two figures occur in the picture, there can be a dialogue between them—and we are almost in the position of dramatic spectators. Finally, as in a dramatic soliloquy, and with exactly the same sort of ambiguity, the pictured figure can address the reader. All of these demand more that an easy acceptance of 'X means Y'; all of them demand an intelligent and thoughtful and evaluating response, which is itself part of the emblem's subject.[99]

Emblem books were complex visual-verbal commonplace books that added a new dimension to the idea of the artificial memory and the idea of topical method. And as such, they enjoyed an almost universal currency. Mosley notes that the commonness of the form as evinced by the many editions of the emblem books, and the readiness with which such editions were translated into other languages, gave it currency as the sign language of Renaissance Europe. [100]

Both Mosley and Yates note the connection of the emblem books with the idea of theater. Mosley comments that the use of visual and verbal discourse in both art forms seems to make that connection inevitable. [101] The emblematists frequently used the trope of the *theatrum mundi*, often referring to their books as theaters in the titles. [102] Emblems were even composed as theater sets; dramatic freeze-frames of symbolic imagery. [103]

In addition to returning to their classical roots as a part of the commonplace tradition, the memory systems of the Renaissance added a new twist to the idea of the interrelatedness of word and thing, that of the microcosm-macrocosm relation between man and cosmos discussed in Chapter 1. Under such a view an orator could speak "from a memory organically affiliated to the proportions of the world harmony." [104] We may take the Renaissance art of memory as an emblem, as it were, of the elements of the ancient and Renaissance world which will enable us to understand Vico's *Scienza nuova* as itself a memory system of no mean proportions. To understand what gives motion and life to the static spaces of Renaissance memory, we need now to consider the dynamics of Aristotelian rhetoric.

6 The Discovery of the
True Aristotle

In many respects the split between logic and rhetoric, whose beginnings I traced in the previous chapter, reached its widest point in Vico's day in the great debate between the Cartesian and baroque theorists over *acutezza*, or *ingenium*. This controversy provided the means for Vico's descent to a genuine Aristotelian rhetoric whose true significance had generally been lost. How did this come about?

Speaking in Conceits

Alessandro Giuliani notes that Vico, like Aristotle, had as a primary concern the relations among rhetoric, logic, and philosophy. This interest made him stand out from "an epoch that had failed to question the legacy of the previous two centuries; rhetoric had emerged from the Renaissance impoverished, once its divorce from logic had been decreed."[1]

Aristotle's account of rhetoric had grown out of an environment of oral praxis, founded in the realities of the juridical and political environment. By Vico's time this "primary rhetoric," which concerned the technē of oral performance, had declined into a "secondary rhetoric," primarily concerned with textual technique.[2] The primacy of secondary rhetoric thus hindered any true appreciation of classical—and specifically Aristotelian—rhetoric.

The central point here is that rhetoric became divorced from the actual situations of juridical or political controversy. Giuliani notes that the tropes and figures of rhetorical theory were not, in classical times, considered mere ornaments of speech; rather, they were developed in response to the exigencies of practical debate. This meant that primary rhetoric was "a technique of presentation, since the choice by the orator must take into account the argumentative situation."[3]

The theory of *status*, or rhetorical controversy, was thus a part of rhetoric as the technē of juridical and political reasoning. In addressing actual situations, such reasoning went beyond merely emotive rhetoric to an art that could distinguish the objective aspects of the problematic situation that needed to be dealt with in a practical manner.[4] The growing emphasis on secondary rhetoric had come to obscure the basic relation between topical thought and judgment that was so evident in the primary rhetoric of the Greeks.

In the baroque-Cartesian debate over ingenium, secondary rhetoric was the unspoken point of reference. The Cartesians asserted that ingenium had at best a decorative function; the epiphenomena of wit could never lead to the truth, as Cartesian method could. Metaphor was deceptive, they felt, because it had no ability to function in a one-to-one correspondence with what it purported to represent: as mere froth on the surface, metaphor was imprecise.[5]

Dominique Bouhours, a leading French critic, wrote in this vein that "thoughts are more or less true to the extent that they more or less conform to their object. The entire conformity constructs what we call the precision of thought, that is to say, just as clothes are well fitted when they are perfectly proportioned to the person who wears them, so thoughts are precise also when they accord perfectly to the things they represent."[6] Metaphors are thus secondary to the primary meaning the metaphor "veils."[7]

In contrast to this, baroque thinkers argued for acutezza (ingenium), which expressed itself organically in metaphors they termed "conceits." Baltasar Gracián, a prominent conceitist, wrote that the conceit "consists in a splendid concordance, in a harmonic correlation between two or more knowable extremes expressed in an act of understanding."[8] As John D. Schaeffer notes, the metaphor or conceit was thought to express with great economy and force the concordance between two apparently dissimilar objects—and the greater the dissimilarity, the greater the power of the conceit. The resulting image then "made sense" to those with the ingenium to see the connection—while appearing to be nonsense to those lacking wit.[9]

The question is, Do these connections express a unique truth that would be distorted if found or expressed in any other way? Gracián claimed that the conceit could be defined as "an act of understanding that expresses the correspondence between things."[10] The baroque theorists thought that this "act of understanding" was unique to the faculty of ingenium, enabling one to achieve a truth that was not obtainable by reason alone. In a conceit, truth is apprehended through a union of logic and style in what Emmanuele Tessauro, following Aristotle, called an *entimemo urbano*, an urbane enthymeme.[11]

But the French critics insisted that what the conceitists called ingenium was merely reason in a figural—and thus less clear and less immediately true—mode. The truth the conceit sought to express was to be found beneath the confusing flash of the wordplay. Logic would be better suited to finding that particular truth anyway; and the logical operations involved in doing so, when "adequately reflected in writing, constituted an aesthetic charm superior to such metaphor."[12]

But if this is the case, as Schaeffer notes, then ingenium is not a faculty separate from reason and has no dignity as an activity that aims at the truth. In addition, "the aesthetic quality of the conceit remain[s] separate from its truth claim, mere icing on the intellectual cake."[13]

But both the baroque theorists and their Cartesian opponents had unconsciously based their reasoning on secondary rhetoric. The overly textual emphasis of the conceitists led them to focus on the literary arts to the exclusion of the practical arena of classical *status*, with its concern for presentation and presence in debate. They were thus unable to answer their critics in any full or satisfying manner. Joseph Mazzeo notes that "the inability to distinguish between the function of metaphor in poetry and the function of metaphor in philosophy and science is at the root of this dilemma."[14] The conceitists could not see such practical distinctions, because they could not see the need to *speak* in conceits. Schaeffer notes that "in Vico's Naples rhetoric was not textually controlled. Rhetoric as Vico knew it, and unlike rhetoric as taught in northern Europe, still aimed at oral performance."[15] Oral performance in the university and the law courts placed a premium on the techniques and practices of primary rhetoric.

In his failed competition for a chair of law at the University of Naples that involved giving a lecture, Vico reports that having reduced his address to a single page of notes, he "delivered it with as much facility as if he had taught nothing else all his life, and with such copiousness of expression as might have served another for a two hours' harangue" (A 163/33).

Vico also reflects this oral milieu in the *Study Methods*, writing that "in pressing, urgent affairs, which do not admit of display or postponement, as most frequently occurs in our law courts—especially when it is a question of criminal cases, which offer to the eloquent orator the greatest opportunity for the display of his powers—it is the orator's business to give *immediate* assistance to the accused, who is usually granted only a few hours in which to plead his defense" (SM 15/799).

As Schaeffer indicates, the pervasiveness of "adversarial oral performance" is essential for understanding Vico's notion of the rhetorical quality of the baroque conceit.[16] The emphasis on the technē of presence—the art of the oral presentation of argumentation in a public manner—is also, I think, one of the keys for understanding how Vico came to appropriate Aristotelian rhetoric and understand the baroque conceit as a gnomic enthymeme.

Vico states in the *Disputation* that "among the Greeks, *rhetores* does not mean those who teach the art, but the 'orators,' who are certainly not to be esteemed as such unless they have acquired that capacity to speak well through which they can defend their causes extemporaneously with eloquence" (R 165/155). This emphasis helps explain why over half of Vico's *Institutes* are devoted to elocution.[17] For Vico, elocution is not simply a stylistic accessory but an intimate concern of the logic of argumentation in real situations. Vico makes the oral performance of elocution primary and, as Giuliani notes, seems to identify it with rhetoric itself.[18] And like classical rhetoric, style is concerned with "the application of words to things."[19]

This is further confirmed by the theory of *status*, or judicial controversy, that we find in the *Institutes*. It is particularly evident in Vico's treatment of *status definitionis*. For Vico, the logical act of defining in the argumentative situation was the main activity of the involved jurists.[20]

Such an activity of definition assumes topical agreements (loci communes) between the participants, and it attempts to address the sensus communis. The rhetorical definitions are then neither real nor nominal but seek to adjust the account (logos, verba) to the probable realities (pragma, res) that are the subject of concern.[21]

Giuliani writes that making such definitions is "an act of human creation, inasmuch as it implies assigning a value to a situation, to a fact."[22] In definition, the *verum-factum* principle comes into play; the true is being made in *status*. And it is the dialectical method, and not scientific demonstration, that affords us definition in the realm of opinion. According to Giuliani, "this is why Vico's reflection on the definition appears to be the point of departure of his principle that the human mind participates in a creative manner in the real. The definition, like the modus operandi of the jurist, is in relation to an order which is not preconstituted but is in a continuous state of self-renewal."[23]

So definitions do not seek to state essences, divorced from probable reality, but instead try to find the limits—and thus the applications—of the topical agreements binding society together. The philosopher must always confront the ordinary cose of philological reality in achieving real human knowledge.[24]

The heart of confronting the ordinary is what Vico calls argument. But, as he notes, "'argument' in this art is not 'the disposition of a proof,' as it is ordinarily understood. . . . Rather, it is that third term that one finds in order to unify the two arguments of a proposed problem, which the Schoolmen call the 'middle term.' Thus, topics is the art that gives us the 'middle term'" (*R* 178/162). This middle term is then identified with the loci of the commonplace tradition. In the *Institutes*, Vico also identifies the third term with the enthymemic maxim.

In a section of the *Institutes* called "De sententiis, vulgo 'del ben parlare in concetti'" (Of maxims; or, of speaking well in conceits), Vico discusses the maxim. There he points to the *ligamen*, the connecting link between words and things that unites them with "enthymemic force" (*IO* 285).[25] The ligamen is, then, the "third thing" that connects apparently disparate objects; it is the middle term, the topos, that ingenium traces out.

The force of the connecting link is the function of an acute wit. Vico writes in *Ancient Wisdom* that "an acute wit penetrates more quickly and unites diverse things, just as two lines are conjoined at the point of an angle below ninety degrees. A wit is obtuse because it penetrates simple things more slowly and leaves diverse things far apart, just as two lines united at a point lie far apart at the base when their angle is greater than ninety degrees" (*AW* 97/117).

In the *Institutes* Vico begins to connect these thoughts with maxims. After discussing Aristotle's division of maxims into four types, he focuses on enthymemic maxims (which, as he states, Aristotle considers superior; *IO* 282–285). He then considers M. Peregrini's account of the maxim. He quotes Peregrini, on the force of wit, which consists in "a rare and novel aptitude to connect two extremes in a very felicitous saying" (*IO* 287).

Vico then connects maxims with metaphors, stating that "in the *Poetics* Aristotle judged that this kind of invention is very difficult, where, in the argument about metaphor, he says it is only with the greatest difficulty and flexibility of wit that proper metaphors are made; and in the *Rhetoric* he writes that only the wisest and most acute philosophers are able to distinguish the likenesses to be seen in different things" (*IO* 286–289).[26]

How, then, does the maxim combine eloquence with logic, beauty with truth? Vico argues against Peregrini, who distinguishes between the intellectual pleasure of a Euclidean demonstration and the pleasure resulting from the acute saying of a poet. According to Peregrini, as Vico quotes him, the demonstration pleases us because the truth accompanies (*assecutos*) it, while the conceit pleases us because we admire its beauty (*pulchrum*; *IO* 292).

This is just the divorce between eloquence and logic I have been discussing. Vico marries them again in the conceit: "When the orator presents a conceit [*acuto dicto*] he makes a beauty that is left for his auditors to detect. For when the conceit is offered, there is indicated within it a rational connection, which, when the hearer traces it out, discovers the middle, unites the extremes, contemplates the aptness, in order to contemplate the beauty the orator made—he then seems ingenious to himself, and the conceit pleases him not as something offered by the orator but as something understood by himself" (*IO* 292).

Schaeffer notes that this description of the conceit is based in primary rhetoric, in the technique of teaching and delighting an audience of listeners. He points out that "the hearer participates in the metaphor when he seizes upon the ligamen and thus unites what is learned with how it is learned. The discovery of this connection is the source of beauty and truth. This act is, for Vico, aural."[27] The audience's reason is called upon just as much as its emotions. The *acuto dicto* (acute saying) is a product of "the specifically philosophic faculty," whose function is to perceive the *ligamen* between dissimilar matters and give them "ingenious, acute, and brilliant forms of expression" (*SM* 24/803).

The key notion here is the situation of *status*, which it is the function of the orator to address and the exigency of which calls forth the conceit (as primal need called forth the archaic metaphors of the first humans). In addressing a problematic situation, the skillful orator does not proceed like a "modern physicist" and lay out the primary axioms first, for this would be to ignore the human realities of the situation (*SM* 25/803). In the art of oratory, Vico notes, "the relationship between speaker and listeners is of the essence" (*SM* 15/799). The realities of the situation being addressed include the human beings to whom the orator is speaking: how they receive truths and how those truths should be communicated.

So the skillful orator, Vico writes, "omits things that are well known, and while impressing on his hearers secondary truth, he tacitly reminds them of the primal points he has left out and while he carries through his argument, his listeners are made to feel they are completing it themselves" (*SM* 25/803).

Since truth must always be remade if it is to be true, the orator does not present a linear, textually oriented account, which proceeds from axiom to axiom in a clear line drawn with an obtuse wit. Through his text, the Cartesian addresses an anonymous audience, which he hopes to incite to a unanimous response. The very flatness and simplicity of the certainties he offers form the basis for that hope.

But to speak to another human being in this way is to demonstrate an appalling ignorance of human reality. Vico notes that "ordering" is a function of prudence, the master art, subordinate to no other. And prudence does not govern by a method or a theory of method; it does not instruct, like artisans do apprentices, "that you do this first, that next, and then the other things in order: this method does not mold a man of practical wisdom, but some type of craftsman" (*AW* 98/117).

Instead, prudence governs topically, enthymemically discerning and uniting apparent opposites through wit. This seems strained, disturbed, and disordered to the Cartesian practitioner. Vico states that "in Demosthenes' disturbed order of speaking, the whole enthymematic capacity of speech is strained like a catapult. For he usually sets forth his argument to give his listeners notice of what is at issue; but soon he is running on about things that seem to have nothing to do with the matter announced" (*AW* 99/118).

The loci of the sensus communis are not univocal or unilinear; they make no sense to the Cartesian practitioner who has become alienated from common life. The tension and organic multivocity of topical thinking seem mad to such a person, as the elements circulate organically through life's common body. For the organic connections—the circulating "middles" which ingenium follows—do not address a linearly linked series of truths. Ingenium instead follows after the topics as they "run about," addressing the whole in terms of the common sense of the human race.

In this process, the acute point at which res and verba combine is in the Aristotelian *gnomē*, or maxim. And as Vico notes, "just as the blood's pulsation may be best studied at the spot where the arterial beat is most perceptible, so the aim of our method of studies shall be treated at the point where it assumes the greatest prominence" (*SM* 6/791). The heartbeat of topical thinking pulses most strongly in the maxim. Vico is now operating, knowingly or unknowingly, in the shadow of Aristotle's *Rhetoric*.

Back to Aristotle

"From whom," Giuliani asks, "could Vico have derived the inspiration for such a conception of rhetoric, which, in a certain sense, was original?"[28] And he answers: From "Aristotle the dialectician, the author of the *Topics*, the *De Sophisticus Elenchis*, the *Rhetoric*, and the *Ethics*."[29]

In his 1701 oration Vico states that his audience should "pay attention to how perceptively Aristotle embraced all the faculties of reasoning. Other philosophers have added nothing to this treatise but some explanations, some arguments and some examples."[30] But his was not an Aristotle recalled in mere nostalgia—a nostalgia that in his view had resulted in the corruption of scholasticism. Vico had no patience for the Aristotle of the Schoolmen; that figure became for him on the one side (as Descartes became on the other) a master metaphor of philosophical degeneration. As he writes, "Today neither the Cartesians nor the *present-day* Aristotelians bring anything useful to oratory" (*IO* 40; emphasis mine).

He was particularly impatient with the Aristotelian physics that came courtesy of the scholastics. Referring to the disrepute in Naples of Aristotelian in favor of Cartesian physics, he writes that the discipline incurred this discredit "on its own account but much more because of the excessive alterations made in it by the schoolmen" (*A* 132/16).

But, as Giuliani notes, Vico found another Aristotle through the topical tradition. He was well aware of how modern rationalism and unthinking nostalgia had obscured genuinely Aristotelian thought (as the two phrases emphasized above indicate).[31] We should be wary of the traditional interpretation that Vico was against Aristotle. I think rather that Vico's growing appropriation of primary rhetoric led him to a genuine understanding of the principles of Aristotle's rhetoric. And regardless of whether he was consciously appropriating Aristotle, he came at this stage of his thought to employ principles found in the "rhetorical" Aristotle. His descent through the tradition is structured by genuine Aristotelian thought.

What is even more interesting is that the understanding Vico shows of Aristotelian rhetoric is not even fully appreciated by most thinkers today. Michael Mooney notes, for example, that Vico is employing the principles of Aristotle the dialectician.[32] But more important than *that* Aristotle, himself a creature of the tradition, artificially split off from the philosopher, is the Aristotle who advocates mastery of the enthymeme. This Aristotle is explored in William J. Grimaldi's studies of the *Rhetoric*. There

Grimaldi argues for a vision of Aristotle, which he claims is startlingly new, that enables us to see the *Rhetoric* as a unified whole.

Grimaldi argues that traditional exegesis of Aristotle's *Rhetoric* goes wrong because it ignores the centrality of the enthymeme. He states that "in actual fact the exegesis of the meaning of *enthumema* not only reveals the specific nature of rhetoric as a *dynamis*, namely something which transcends all particular disciplines, but also the complete relevance of *ethos* and *pathos* and the whole complex of *psychagogia* in his theory of rhetoric."[33]

What is interesting is the way the Aristotles of Grimaldi and Vico converge. And the point at which they converge most acutely is in the idea of the maxim, which as an enthymeme is something far more than the familiar abbreviated syllogism of the tradition. What then is an enthymeme? What is its unique status in Aristotle's rhetoric? How is the enthymeme related to the maxim? Why is it so important for Vico that we become, like Demosthenes, masters of enthymemes? And how can the idea of the enthymeme give us a crucial perspective on Vico's path of descent to archaic mentality and help us envisage a model for the Vichian axiom?

The Body of Persuasion

The traditional critique of rhetoric is well known. Grimaldi sums it up well when he writes that "as an academic discipline rhetoric has long been identified exclusively with the facile manipulation of language. We find this view reflected in every phase of contemporary critical activity. Prose, poetry, painting, politics, and philosophy are dismissed as 'rhetorical' when the criticism is to underscore concentration on form with little or no reference to content."[34] What is less well understood is Aristotle's response to this critique.

Aristotle's *Rhetoric* has confused traditional scholarship because traditional scholars approach the text in the belief that *rhetoric* is already understood. They do not view Aristotle's text as something strange and unfamiliar but instead read it with the QED ready to hand. For this reason, they have not "unthought the obvious"—and thus recognized the function of the enthymeme in Aristotle's rhetoric. They have failed to see that "the enthymeme as the main instrument of rhetorical argument incorporates the interplay of reason and emotion in discourse."[35]

The central mistake made by traditional scholars stems from a misunderstanding of the relation between the *pisteis* (means of persuasion) and the *enthumema:* making the enthymeme one of the three available means of persuasion, these scholars take the further step of identifying the enthymeme with a solely logical demonstration. What does this mean?

In Book I of the *Rhetoric* Aristotle says: "Let rhetoric be defined as an ability to see concerning each individual case the possible means of persuasion" (*Rh* 1355b25–26).[36] And like dialectic, of which it is the correlative (*antistrophē*), it is not confined to its own particular subject area, as are the other arts (including medicine and geometry).[37] Aristotle states that "rhetoric seems, so to speak, to be able to see the persuasive concerning the given" (*Rh* 1355b34–35). It deals with the "givens" of any situation.

Aristotle then distinguishes between *atechnoi*, or inartistic means of persuasion, and *entechnoi*, or artistic ones. The inartistic are what circumstance gives us to deal with, while the artistic pisteis are "whatever can be constructed through method and by us" (*Rh* 1355b38).

There are then three main types of artistic pisteis, "for some are in the character of the one speaking, and some in somehow disposing the listener, and some in the rational significance" (1356a1–4). The traditional interpretation is to identify the three artistic pisteis as ethos, pathos, and enthumēma, and to further identify an enthymeme as simply an abbreviated syllogism.[38]

But this is to misconstrue the text. The key term is the third of the artistic pisteis, which is specified as being found "in the logos itself." As Grimaldi points out, this phrase need not be taken to refer exclusively to syllogistic inference and thus to the enthymeme (setting aside for the moment the larger issue of what a rhetorical enthymeme is). It can (and should) be taken to refer to the explanation of the subject viewed in its logical aspect, that is, "its internal, rational coherence and significance."[39]

The rational means of persuasion concern the "logical matter" of the subject under consideration, making it only one of three aspects of rhetorical discourse. What the phrase "in the logos itself" indicates is then "something like *to pragma*, and signifies the subject of discourse in its purely logical character, which speaks to the intellect of the auditor, just as *ēthos* and *pathos* are aspects connected with the subject which transmit significance to his emotions, feelings, and will."[40]

Aristotle clearly states in the first section of the *Rhetoric* that the enthymeme "is the body of persuasion" (1354a15), and that the subject of the artistic pisteis concerns "how one goes about becoming master of the enthymeme" (1355b22). He nowhere states that the enthymeme is one of the three artistic pisteis.[41]

All of this is significant because the traditional interpretation, by identifying the enthymeme with one of the three artistic pisteis, then taking Aristotle at his word that the enthymeme was the center of rhetorical activity, and then, moreover, identifying the enthymeme with an abbreviated syllogism, had both overintellectualized Aristotle and convicted him of contradiction at the same time. For if Aristotle "conveys the impression that the art of rhetoric for him pertains exclusively to the intellect and concerns itself quite simply with merely the logical proof of the subject under discussion," and then immediately after this "admits *ēthos* and *pathos* as elements co-equal with reason in the art of rhetoric, it would seem that we would more reasonably inquire whether or not this position is possible for him."[42]

But if the enthymeme is not the instrument of reason alone but rather the "integrating structure of rhetorical discourse," then it involves three correlative "proofs," respectively involving logos, pathos, and ēthos, each of which is necessary to organic discourse. For "just as the scientific syllogism organizes the sources of knowledge, so the rhetorical syllogism can organize the sources of conviction."[43] And the "rational matters" the enthymeme organizes make up just one part of a coordinate whole.

This understanding fits in quite well with the task of the rhetorician that Aristotle is investigating. The rhetorician seeks to bring other human beings to a *krisis*, a judgment. And since any oral discourse explicitly involves other persons, as either audience or interlocutors, "we must accept the fact that the person as an integral entity enters into reasoned discussion. As a totality of intellect, will, and emotions, he approaches and attempts to resolve the problematic thesis placed before him."[44]

Apodeixis rhetorikē (rhetorical demonstration) as enthymeme is, then, one of "the artistic ways of proceeding concerning the means of persuasion" (*Rh* 1355a4). The other is *paradeigma*, paradigm. Aristotle states that just as in dialectic there is *epagōgē* (induction) on the one hand and syllogism on the other, so in rhetoric there is paradigm and enthymeme. Paradigm is the antistrophē, the counterpart or correlative, in rhetoric to the induction from particulars in dialectic, as enthymeme is the correlative to the syllogism (*Rh* 1356b1–10).

But the emphasis in the *Rhetoric* is on the enthymeme. It is given priority as the "the body of persuasion" (*Rh* 1354a15). What precisely then is an enthumēma? What is its function? And how does it relate to topical method?

The Invincible Enthymeme

Aristotle distinguishes in the *Topics* between different types of syllogism: a philosopheme (apodeictic); an epicheireme (dialectical); a sophisma (eristic); and an aporeme (dialectical and concluding to a contradiction).[45] As Grimaldi notes, Aristotle was careful with his terminology, minutely distinguishing this from that. So in the light of the passage above, one wonders why he choose *enthumēma* to mean a rhetorical syllogism. If an epicheireme, for example, is an inference from probabilities, we might expect that "when Aristotle calls rhetorical inference which argues from probabilities an enthymeme he has some further purpose in mind."[46]

As I noted earlier, Aristotle's customary method was to work within the context of tradition, transforming its concepts from within.[47] A look at the use of the term *enthymeme* prior to Aristotle is, as Grimaldi points out, called for.

The traditional way to interpret *enthymeme* in works preceding Aristotle is as a "thought." But this is to ignore the clear distinctions between *thumos* and its cognates and those of *noos* (mind): *enthumeomai* and *ennoeomai, enthumēma* and *ennoēma*, and *enthumēmatikos* and *en-noēmatikos*, and so forth.[48] Grimaldi states that "to have something *en thumō* is not simply to 'have a thought.' The use of the word *thumos* in the literature as the principle of feeling and thought does not permit such a precisive identity with 'thought' as has been made."[49]

The principal definition of *thumos* is "the principle of life, feeling and thought, esp. of strong feeling and passion."[50] It is a term that indicates the mixed nature of the force motivating human action, and it thus refers to the seat of desire and emotion, as well as to thought. It is therefore often translated as "heart," and to have something *en thumō* can mean to "take it to heart."[51]

The evidence suggests that when Aristotle came to pick a word for his specifically rhetorical syllogism, he chose a term from the tradition that suggested an act not simply of noos, mind, but of the whole person as an organism of intellect and emotion.[52]

Aristotle's signal contribution was to understand rhetoric as a technē that structured discourse through syllogizing but that did so in such a way that "in the effort to effect judgement and decision whose conse-quences involve the one judging, and further to do this in the area of the probable and contingent, one must seek out as sources to convince not only the rational explanation of the subject (*pragma*) but also the emotive ele-ments in the subject (*ēthos* and *pathos*)."[53] He chose a word that reflected this awareness.

Enthymeme, then, signifies an organic act of discourse involving the complete reality of the audience, the orator, and the situation. How are we to understand the operation of the rhetorical syllogism in the light of topical method?

Aristotle writes: "I mean dialectical and rhetorical syllogisms to be those concerning which we state topics" (*Rh* 1358a10–12). He adds that topics can be either general or particular. General topics apply to any species of knowledge, while particular topics are specific to the field of knowledge to which they relate. In terms of rhetoric, the topics are the sources for the premises of enthymemes and are thus sources for discourse structured by enthymeme in the activity of effecting persuasion (*Rh* 1358a15–35).[54]

The key difference between general and particular topics is that particular topics offer the material, or *hule*, which the general topics structure. The particular topics, as Grimaldi puts it, "present one with sources, or focal points, to be examined in order that one may derive all . . . the varied particular aspects of an individual subject which can throw light upon the subject for the audience and the field of knowledge which it represents."[55] The sources are brought into focus, as it were, through the general topics.

The general topics represent the ways into which the mind naturally falls when it starts to think about particulars. Grimaldi states that "as general axiomatic propositions they are valid forms of inference by themselves. Further, they may also be applied to the subject-matter presented by the *eidē* [particular topics] to permit one to reason by enthymeme with this material."[56] They are the "properties of the human mind" that determine how we think about what we are presented with.

The heart of common topics is that they connect diverse particulars in a quick and comprehensive manner. Grimaldi writes that "they always assume a form of reasoning which leads the mind from one thing to another."[57] In this, according to Aristotle, the mode of comprehension peculiar to the enthymeme is like the metaphor in that it "brings before the eyes" (*Rh* 1411b23) and "makes the lifeless living" (*Rh* 1411b32) through connecting opposites. For as he notes, "as in philosophy, too, it is characteristic of a well-aimed mind to see the likeness even in widely separated things" (*Rh* 1412a12–13).

This means that the antithetic style, which sets two things side by side, is the essence of enthymeme. Aristotle writes of antithesis that it "is the 'home' of the enthymeme" (*Rh* 1401a6–7). He also states that the preferred enthymemes consist in "the bringing together of opposites in brief form" (*Rh* 1400b27). Aristotle, like Vico, is a partisan of the acute.

This relates to his prescription that enthymemes be condensed as much as possible (*Rh* 1419a19) but need not refer to the famous "mutilated syllogism" of the tradition (which takes the heart of enthymeme to be the fact that it is a syllogism with a suppressed premise).[58] There is here, as Grimaldi notes, "a definite predilection for enthymeme as a brief, direct and compact inference, and possibly (not necessarily) in an abbreviated form. The reason for this attitude of Aristotle is determined by the factor which always plays a key role in his analysis of rhetoric: the audience."[59]

Aristotle is here concerned with what Cicero would characterize as the res and verba of the situation: word and reality should be organically related in discourse. He is concerned to integrate the pragma, "those rational probabilities, opinions, truths about the subject which translate it to the mind as reasonable"; the ēthos, the personal elements of speaker and auditor that concern the style of discourse "as it is affected by and flows into the subject-matter"; and the pathos, "the interplay of feeling, sensibility, emotions in relation to the subject of discourse."[60]

Aristotle writes that "I mean by 'element' and 'topic' the same thing" (*Rh* 1403a17). This calls to mind, as Grimaldi notes, Theophrastus' definition of *topos* as "some sort of governing root or element."[61] These elements or principal roots are not static storehouses of the tradition—places where arguments reside or hide and we go to hunt them up. Aristotle has taken the traditional terminology (curiously enough, the traditional terminology of both before *and* after him) and given it a dynamic sense.

The general topics circulate among the particulars, organizing them with enthymemic force. This involves not only invention—the art of finding the place of the argument—but the *energeia* (activity) of *mathēsis tacheia* (swift learning). Topical methodology, like metaphor, "makes all things to move and live—and energeia is motion" (*Rh* 1412a10). The motive force of this energeia is what Vico called ingenium, which propels the topics like blood through the body of discourse. Recall Vico's comment that "just as the blood does in animate bodies, so will these elements course through our science and animate it in all its reasonings" (119).

The general and particular topics operate in tandem to bring witty focus to the subject under consideration. As Grimaldi puts it, Aristotle brings activity into topical method through enlarging the static "case methodology" of the topic. A topic as a static locale for an argument is brought into activity through the introduction of the general topics. He did this because of his awareness "that anything—particularly anything in the area of the probable which is the primary subject-matter of rhetoric—may be conditioned and altered by its situation."[62]

The general topics, or elements, circulate like blood through the body of the situation, organizing particulars into general patterns that reflect the pragma, ēthos, and pathos of the realities under consideration. This organization becomes particularly clear in Aristotle's discussion of the maxim.

Aristotle states that "a maxim is a statement (not, however, about things taken singly) . . . but of a general sort, not about all things . . . but about things concerning actions, and [these things] are those things chosen or avoided in acting" (*Rh* 1394a21-25). A maxim concerns prudential action in the realm of human probabilities, addressing itself in a general way to the possibilities of action in a particular situation. The maxim is a matter of practical wisdom.

The maxim is intimately involved with what Aristotle termed *proairesis*, or "moral choice." *Proairesis* primarily means "choosing one thing before another," although it came to signify "preference" or "deliberate choice."[63] Aristotle enriched this traditional term to include the notion of a moral choice that involves a rational choice or deliberate preference for the good.[64] In making such a choice one creates a context of values in terms of means and ends ordered toward the highest good chosen. The person with *aretē*, moral excellence, will choose the good as it appears in the particular situation through an intimate intersection of character, upbringing, emotion, and rationality.[65] Reflecting this, *proairesis* could also mean "expressed opinion or advice" concerning how to choose.[66] A proairesis coalesces into a maxim.

Aristotle writes that in using maxims in oratory, "one should make the moral choice altogether clear in its style or arrangement" (*Rh* 1395a27–28). In doing so the maxim makes the speech *ēthikous* (ethical) —it relates it to the complex of character, emotion, upbringing, and rationality, revealing each of these in turn in both speaker and audience (*Rh* 1395b13–14, 1395a24–25, 1395b10ff.).[67] Given this characterization of maxims, Aristotle notes: "Consequently, since the enthymeme is like a syllogism concerning these things, maxims are more or less the conclusions of enthymemes or the premises taken away from the syllogism" (*Rh* 1394a25–28).

The first thing to notice about this passage is the phrase "like a syllogism *concerning these things*." "These things, of course," refers to the moral nexus described above. Grimaldi takes this passage to be confirmation that the enthymeme is not an epicheireme but must be thought of in other than strictly logical terms.[68] And this is why, Aristotle says, the maxim is like an enthymeme: it reflects the complex issue involved in moral choice.

Second, the premises and the conclusions are often gnomic in character. We should relate this notion to Aristotle's division of maxims into four types, based upon the division between those "with the 'supplementary reason'" and those "without the 'supplementary reason'" (*Rh* 1394b8). A maxim with the supplementary reason is either part of an enthymeme, or enthymematic but not a part of an enthymeme (*Rh* 1394b17,20). A maxim without the supplementary reason is either already understood beforehand (that is, common knowledge), or clear upon being spoken (sufficiently obvious; *Rh* 1394b11,14–15). Maxims without supplementary reason can be converted into enthymemes through the addition of the "reason." Maxims are not ranked separately as methods of artistic proof, along with paradigm and enthymeme, for the pivotal fact is that "the maxim is part of an enthymeme" (*Rh* 1393a21–23).

Enthymemes can then become more or less gnomic, ranging from an epicheiremic extreme that is practically dialectic to the gnomic apotheosis of moral choice and common sense. As Grimaldi notes, this distinction was clear to the ancient commentators on Aristotle. Planudes cites the first or second century BCE "technographer" Neocles, who wrote that "the syllogism is constructed from premises and a conclusion; but the enthymeme as compared with the epicheireme is born 'compressed' with one axiom of ēthos and one of pathos, and sometimes the two are mixed up together."[69]

This statement relates to Aristotle's comment that "strictly logical demonstration has neither ēthos nor moral choice" (*Rh* 1418a16–17). He adds that this is why maxims should be used in narration and persuasion— because they are "ethical" (*Rh* 1418a18). As the enthymeme becomes more gnomic, its mixed character, to which Neocles referred, becomes emphasized; it enters more and more into the sensus communis, becoming a part of common life.

Aeschines stated: "I believe that we learn the maxims of poets carefully when we are children for this reason, that we may use them when we are men."[70] The maxim is received through custom and education, through memory and attention to its eloquence; it then shows its "reason" in the informed and deliberate choices of social life. The gnomic enthymeme combines heart and reason through the "very well-regulated excess" (*AR* 87/939) of organic rhetorical discourse. It addresses the whole and is thus as essential element in the discourse of *sapienza che parla:* wisdom speaking. As such, it is the antithesis of the abstract analytic method of the new mathematical sciences, to which Vico opposes his own new science.

7 The Comic Nature of Geometric Method

New sciences have always been associated with a revival of mathematics—at least, in modern thought. The applications of mathematical and geometrical method to the knowledge of motion in the Renaissance revival of mathematics is a case in point. This revival gave us not only the *Nova Scientia* (1537) of Niccolò Tartaglia but also the more famous *Discorsi e dimostrazioni matematiche, intorno a due nuove scienze attenti alla mecanica e i movimenti locali* (1638) of Galileo.

The common feature of Renaissance schemes like these is a method for representing mechanical forces and motions through geometrical representations.[1] Their distinctive gesture is the ritual bow to Euclid through the rubrics of his geometry: axioms, definitions, postulates, and demonstrations. Their common ēthos is optimism.

The Prestige and Optimism of Geometry

The new sciences adhered to the geometrical terminology not only because of the great prestige of Euclid but because of their development from the revival of ancient mathematics. Their key attitude demonstrated respect for the rigor and certainty of mathematics as epitomized in geometry and an optimistic belief that its supposed necessity could be transferred to other realms of human activity. Descartes summed up this attitude well when he wrote that "arithmetic and geometry alone are free from any taint of falsity or uncertainty. . . . In our inquiry for the right way to attain truth, we should occupy ourselves with no objective about which we cannot arrive at a certainty equal at least to that reached in the demonstrations of arithmetic and geometry."[2]

It was this index of necessity, along with its applicability to the "real" world, that gave geometry its allure and fundamental optimism. For geometry could apparently be applied not only to imaginary space but to the "real space" of natural motions in a way that seemed entirely consistent. Edwin Arthur Burtt notes that Euclid seemingly took for granted the notion that geometrical and physical space coincided and that "our current conception of mathematics as an ideal science, of geometry in particular as dealing with an ideal space, rather than an actual space in which the universe is set, was a notion quite unformulated before Hobbes, and not taken seriously till the middle of the eighteenth century."[3]

The intersection of the idea of necessity with the revival of geometric method, and the optimistic application of this idea to "local space," is epitomized in one of the first "new sciences," that of Niccolò Tartaglia, the sixteenth-century mathematician and physicist who did much to lay the groundwork for the developing sciences of motion. Tartaglia's *Nova Scientia*, or *New Science*, was part of his general program for a renewal of mathematics that was based upon a new reading of the classical texts of Euclid and Archimedes, which he translated in 1543. In his introduction to the translation of Euclid he wrote that in his day "mathematics has not only been corrupted by the *moderni* but so annulled that the mathematical sciences are almost completely lost."[4]

In his *New Science* Tartaglia essayed a mathematical method for dealing with dynamics and motion based upon his understanding of the ancient texts. In this work he presages the better-known work of Giambattista Benedetti and Galileo.[5] Paul Lawrence Rose notes that "in its very layout the *Nova Scientia* marks a departure from medieval treatises on motion. It is arranged, *more geometrico*, in the form of definitions, suppositions, axioms, and presuppositions."[6] And the subject of Tartaglia's "demonstrations" was not motion in general but "only a treatment of the specific case of the movement of those projectiles minimally affected by air-resistance."[7] Through his method Tartaglia optimistically set out to solve the puzzles of local motion.

The conjunction of the renewal of mathematics with an application to an analysis of local motion was carried on by Tartaglia's pupil Benedetti (1530–1590). Benedetti's optimistic goal was to import the necessity of geometrical analysis into the physical investigations of motion.

As Rose puts it, for Benedetti, "where this method of *philosophia* or *speculatio mathematica* was successfully applied, the new science was given an unshakable foundation."[8] The problem Benedetti faced was excessive adherence to the letter of ancient geometry at the expense of the spirit of the new science, which sometimes led his analyses of particular physical problems astray. This problem was resolved by Galileo.[9] For Galileo, the point at issue in the mathematical revival was the need to follow the constraints of method apart from any strict adherence to the strictures of the past; to do whatever would maintain necessity—the hallmark of mathematics in its applications to the science of local space.

In his *Discourse on Bodies in Water* (1611–12), for example, Galileo tried to resolve various physical problems through a "purely Archimedean" geometric method.[10] He found that he would have to modify the "rigorously geometrical method of Archimedes" in order to "unify dynamics and statics into a new science of mechanics."[11] The important thing was to maintain the element of certainty in the analysis, rather than the continuity with the tradition that had plagued his predecessors.

In this way the methodology, in its concrete application, was modified—but the terminology of Euclid, and the emphasis on certainty and necessity, remained in full force. The remarkable discoveries and achievements of the new physics—which resulted in the tremendous prestige of such figures as Galileo, Descartes, and Newton—were expressed through the rubrics of ancient geometry. Yet the course the new sciences took in their development brought them farther and farther from the strictly Euclidean roots of spatial representation.

The move from Euclid is most clearly seen in the growing use of algebraic symbols by the "new geometers," a use that freed them from a cumbersome dependence on spatial representation.[12] With Descartes's invention of analytic geometry, the new sciences received an invaluable tool in their quest for certainty.

Descartes saw that in the new physics space itself must be thought of in such a way that its relations could be expressed numerically, and numerical relations in turn could be spatially expressed.[13] This meant, as Burtt notes, that "the whole realm of physics might be reducible to geometrical qualities alone. Whatever else the world of nature may be, it is obviously a geometrical world, its objects are extended and figured magnitudes in motion. If we can get rid of all other qualities, or reduce them to these, it is clear that mathematics must be the sole and adequate key to unlock the truths of nature."[14] This gave the Renaissance geometrical quest for necessity enormous impetus.

The rejection of the image, and the bodily basis of thought, is a key element in the development of the new method. The data of the mathematical sciences become, as Beck puts it, "absolutely simple and precise . . . arithmetic and geometry in point of fact, consist entirely in the logical development of these data by an inference from self-evident data to conclusions linked and interconnected at each stage by steps which are themselves self-evident."[15]

Only what is clearly presented to the mind's inspection as indubitable can be trusted—and the senses are not indubitable. The mathematical sciences thus need not consider anything intrinsic to sense experience, so their certainty is not subject to empirical verification.[16] Ann Hartle notes that "the method is presented as mathematical in character, but this is a mathematics that is subtly freed from the imagination and thus from the body."[17]

To decrease the dependence on the imagination and the body, Descartes first used lines for his mathematics, for lines seem simpler to the senses. He next made the move to algebraic symbols, in his *Geometry*.[18] Hartle notes that "what is made to appear as a matter of mere convenience is in fact the elimination of the imagination from mathematical thought."[19] Geometric method, so conceived, seeks above all to escape the strictures of memory.

Memory, for Descartes, represents an essential limitation on the operation of the intellect in its primary functioning, for memory is a bodily, and so a contingent, activity. When one follows the chain of interlinked deductions that are so crucial to the new method, it may become so long that one need rely on memory to keep the intermediate steps in mind.

But if this is true, then we are not really knowing while we are remembering, for knowledge is by definition an immediate intuition. To deduce something, and to know it, "means to arrive at it by passing from link to link of the whole chain with a continuous and unbroken movement of thought. "[20] To bring in the body with memory is to cloud the intellectual vision of the simple natures that present themselves clearly and indubitably to the mind. Memory and imagination are simply contingent limitations on the operation of the intellect.

The key idea here is to minimize the role of memory as much as possible, using such aids as the method of enumeration. In Rule 11 of the *Regulae* Descartes states that we need to run through the deductive steps repeatedly, "until I pass so quickly from the first step to the last that for all practical purposes nothing is left to memory and I seem to view the whole all at the same time. "[21] One prescinds from the contingencies of the body as much as possible. The goal is to become a disembodied mind, a thinking thing. [22]

In the new sciences of the dawning modern era, the new methods of analyses that rejected memory and the image in favor of deductive analysis were clothed in the language of ancient geometry. The fantastic results of this method were also clothed in the language of Euclid, giving that terminology enormous prestige. "Geometrical method" was to the dawning modern age akin to what computer science is to ours; one need only employ its "methods" and make the ritual bow to its rubrics to be certified as genuinely scientific and progressive.

Vico states that when he returned to Naples in 1723 he found that the physics of Descartes was the rage, "at the height of its renown among the established men of letters" (*A* 132/16). He further notes that according to "our scientists, that type of physics which they teach, based on the geometrical method, is, as it were, the authentic voice of Nature. Wherever you turn in contemplating the universe, you will constantly be met by the ever-present modern physics" (*SM* 21/802). Wherever Vico turned, he was met with the prestige and optimism of the new geometry. How did Vico respond to the claims of the new method? How he did he react to its optimistic claims of necessity and its seemingly unlimited possibility as a tool of reform?

Eugenio Garin notes that Vico was "aware of every voice in the Europe of his time that reject[ed] the exasperating quantification of Hobbes and Spinoza: the passions as forces that can be added and subtracted like numbers and geometrical figures. "[23] Instead of joining with the voices, Vico stepped outside their nostalgia to offer a novel science, which countered the arrogant optimism of the new sciences that had called forth the nostalgic reaction. His key move was to locate the necessity that all these new sciences thought worth thinking as based only on a partial understanding of human knowing. He offered a new analysis of knowledge in place of the analysis of the new sciences, one which offered consequences that were uncongenial to the optimistic orientation of the mathematico-deductive method.

According to Vico, a method, or *ratio*, is made up of instruments (*instrumenta*), complementary aids (*adiumenta*), and an end (*finis* or *telos*). The instruments embody the heart of the method, for they "presuppose and include a systematic, orderly way of proceeding" (*SM* 6/793). Instruments prepare one for the task of learning, while the aids are concomitant with it—and the ends guide the whole process.

Vico states that the new critique (*nova critica*) is the common instrument of all the modern arts and sciences, while the instrument of geometry is analysis (*geometriae analysis; SM* 6/793). By *critica* Vico means Cartesian method and by *analysis*, the analytical geometry of Descartes that combined algebra and geometry in illustration of the analytic method.[24]

According to Vico the fundamental claim of geometrical analysis is found in its application to physics. Writing ironically of the new scientists and how they view themselves, he states that "holding to this method as to Ariadne's thread . . . they can reach the end of their appointed journey. Do not consider them as groping practitioners of physics: they are to be viewed, instead, as the grand architects of this limitless fabric of the world: able to give a detailed account of the ensemble of principles according to which God has built this admirable structure of the cosmos" (*SM* 9–10/795). Their method is all of a piece, centered around the subtle linear links of the deductive chain. And what drives the method is its enormous confidence and optimism: "Our scientists" think that their physics "is, as it were, the authentic voice of nature" (*SM* 21/802). And if the "structure and function" of the universe are exactly as these scientists claim, we owe them our thanks. But is their optimism justified?

For Vico, the method of lock-step deduction is well suited to the mathematical field; but for a field of studies that is not consonant with it, "the geometrical procedure may be a faulty and captious way of reasoning" (*SM* 23/803). This is especially true of physics.

As I pointed out in Chapter 2, for Vico, "we are able to demonstrate geometrical propositions because we create them; were it possible for us to supply demonstrations of propositions of physics, we would be capable of creating them *ex nihilo* as well" (*SM* 23/803). But we only *witness* the elements of the natural world—we have no maker's knowledge of them. However clearly we see the elements, however certain we are of their arrangement, we possess no maker's knowledge of them but merely reflect upon them as given to the witnessing consciousness. We do not join two dissimilar things with acute wit, creating beautiful connections in human making; rather, we obtusely link the witnessed elements together in a linear series.

What are optimistically presented as clear and distinct portraits of reality on the authority of geometric method are then "not really truths, but wear a semblance of probability" (*SM* 23/803). A metaphysics compatible with human frailty sees that we are mere witnesses in the natural cosmos, which was indeed created—but not by us.

Vico states that real method operates silently: when it makes a lot of noise, something is out of kilter (*R* 181/165). The *moderni* are shouting in the dark, because "they do not believe there is any light save where it is reflected" (*R* 170/158). So there is all the noise of axioms, definitions, postulates, and method as the moderns jostle one another, making blatant claims of having accurately limned the cosmos. Opposing such reflection, Vico writes, "It is our task to study physics in a speculative temper of mind, as philosophers, that is, curbing our presumption" (*SM* 23/803).

If there is no room for the optimism of geometry in the (humanly) uncreated realm, what about in the realm of what we do create? How are we to understand the true, the certain, and the made in relation to the world of humans, where Vico came to find the scienza that eluded the grasp of the moderni? Do we find an optimism corresponding to that of the Cartesian method in his geometry of nations?

The Certain, the True, and the Made

In his introduction to the *Scienza nuova*, the "Explanation of the Picture Placed as a Frontispiece to Serve as an Introduction to the Work," Vico points out that his work embodies a new critical art in which "philosophy undertakes to examine philology" (7). He also states in axiom X that "philosophy contemplates reason, whence comes knowledge of the true, philology observes that of which human choice is author, whence comes consciousness of the certain" (138). In the corollary to this axiom he adds, "This same axiom shows how the philosophers failed by half in not giving certainty to their reasonings by appeal to the authority of the philologians, and likewise how the latter failed by half in not taking care to give their authority the sanction of truth by appeal to the reasonings of the philosophers. If they had done this they would have been more useful to their commonwealths and *they would have anticipated us in conceiving this science*" (140; emphasis mine).

Finally, in the "Establishment of Principles" Vico divides his general axioms into those that are refutative (I-IV), and those that provide the foundation of the true and the foundation of the certain (163). These passages show that the mainspring of the methodology of the new science rests upon the relation between the certain and the true, not upon a simple epistemological extrapolation from the verum-factum principle of his earlier works.[25]

Vico first came upon the relation between the certain and the true through his study of law. He writes in the *Autobiography* that when he began to study law, one of the things that he took a great pleasure in was "seeing how, in their summaries of the laws, the scholastic interpreters had abstracted in general maxims of justice the particular considerations of equity which the jurisconsults and emperors had indicated for the just dispositions of cases" (*A* 116/7).

The Pandects of Justinian were for Vico a model of such a fusion of universal and particular. He writes in the *Study Methods* that in the Pandects one does not find an "art of the law," for law had not yet become artificially separated from philosophy: "There is only one 'art' of prudence, and this art is philosophy" (*SM* 48/823). Calling upon Horace, he notes that "the same definition served the Romans for jurisprudence and the Greeks for wisdom: 'the knowledge of things human and divine'" (*SM* 49/823).

Guido Fassò notes that the phrase "new science" first occurs in Vico in conjunction with a consideration of the universal and the particular in law. It is found in the second part of *De constantia jurisprudentis*, entitled "De constantia philologiae." There, Vico adds a short introductory comment to a section called "Nova scientia tentatur" (A new science is essayed).[26] There Vico states that "since, moreover, the human being consists of intellect and will, everything the human being knows is derived from the intellect or will of the human being; and everything that is called knowledge refers either to the necessity of reason or the will of authority. Philosophy confirms the constancy of reason: let us try to confirm the constancy of authority, inasmuch as we have said that authority is a part of reason [qua via diximus auctoritatem partem esse rationis]."[27]

Scienza, maker's knowledge, finds its true arena in considering the causes of the human world. Vico writes in axiom IX that "men who do not know what is true of things take care to hold fast to what is certain, so that, if they cannot satisfy their intellects by maker's knowledge their wills at least may rest on witnessing consciousness" (137). The certain that the human individual qua individual did not make can be seen in the laws that have been made in the past by human will or authority. Not made by the individual, but nonetheless made by humans, the laws are not a product of the divine will. They are only contingently "flat" to me, unlike the created world of nature, which will always necessarily lack for the individual knower (qua human) the three dimensions of maker's knowledge.

Vico writes in axiom XI that "human choice, by its nature most uncertain, is made certain and determined by the common sense of men with respect to human needs or utilities, which are the two sources of the natural law of the gentes" (141). He further states in axiom CV that "the natural law of the gentes is coeval with the customs of the nations, conforming one with another in virtue of a common human sense" (311).

Particular human needs result in particular customs, which are then certain for the historical witness. When we examine the realm of the certain in philology, which includes "the study of languages and the deeds of peoples" (139), we are witnesses to acts of human making, which as modifications of the human mind can then be remade by us. Donald Phillip Verene notes that "the things of the civil world are made by men. . . . They arise through acts of human will that confront other past and present acts of human will. The human world as made always confronts the human world as it has been made and is being made."[28]

This means that the certain is a part of the true in the new science, just as a particular law was a specific determination of universal justice in Vico's study of jurisprudence. Every historical particular to which I am witness is potentially convertible to the intelligibility of maker's knowledge.

When the philological is converted to the philosophical, and we have maker's knowledge of all things human, where is the other half of wisdom—the knowledge of things divine—to be found? I now want to claim that if the certain is part of the true, then that thing of which we can only be certain is part of the made. What does this mean?

It should be obvious from the account I have been giving that nature, as created by God, is clearly something of which we can only be certain, and it is a part of the made that is uncreated by humans. But what happens when we recover the cose which have made us human? Is there something underlying that creative act?

Vico states that one of the principal aspects of his science is that it is a "rational civil theology of divine providence, which seems hitherto to have been lacking" (342). It was lacking because when earlier philosophers looked at human things, they erred in their account of these cose in one of three characteristic ways: like the Epicureans, they explained cose as "a blind concourse of atoms"; like the Stoics, they explained them through "a deaf chain of cause and effect"; or like natural theologians, they ended up with God as a final cause—which merely explained the motions of the natural universe rather than human realities (342).

What these three types of thinkers ignore is providence. Vico writes that they "ought to have studied it in the economy of civil institutions, in keeping with the full meaning of applying to providence the term 'divinity' [that is, the power of divining], from *divinari*, to divine, which is to understand what is hidden *from* men—the future—or what is hidden *in* men—their consciousness" (342). It is this, Vico adds, that makes up one of the principal subjects of jurisprudence: the divine cose, of which human cose are a part (342).

When we convert the philological particulars that make up the human world to the universals of maker's knowledge, we find them intelligible as human things. We have their causes within ourselves as humans and can narrate them to ourselves *per causas*. In this way we perform what Vico calls logical proofs, which have as their complement "the sublime natural theological proofs" of divine providence (346). When we reason "logically," according to the logos of the origins, we are reasoning about the archai of the cose, and "we reach those first beginnings beyond which it is vain curiosity to demand others earlier. . . . We explain the particular ways in which they came into being; that is to say, their nature, the explanation of which is the distinguishing mark of science" (346).

When we perform these "logical proofs" in converting the "certains" as humanly made into the "trues" of maker's knowledge, a pattern inevitably emerges that has a twofold aspect. First, inasmuch as the certains we convert are products of human making, we invariably find in them the three principles of religion, marriage, and burial. These principles, which inform all society as a part of human making, allow us to discern an intelligible structure in the diverse particular customs of the nations. These structures result from the logical proofs that articulate the logos of the origin.

Second, the *way* a nation develops from these origins is not something made by humans; the pattern of the development cannot be converted into maker's knowledge. So Vico writes of the aspect of his science that concerns providence: "Our new science must therefore be a demonstration, so to speak, of what providence has wrought in history, for it must be a history of the things by which, without human discernment or counsel, and often against the designs of men, providence has ordered this great city of the human race" (342).

The temporal pattern of the development of human cose is not intelligible in terms of maker's knowledge. As a *storia ideale eterna*, it is a pattern we witness when we perform the act of converting every possible philological certain into a true of maker's knowledge. It "resists" our "knowledge-making" activity. It is here that we begin to learn our learned ignorance.

As I discussed in Chapter 4, the master image of the ideal eternal history, which embodies a process that begins in necessity and ends in madness, is analogous to the master image of Jove in the experience of the first human beings. And as the physical thunder was to the first humans, so is history to the "new seer" who is the Vichian scientist.

To divine, Vico told us in the passage quoted above, is to understand what is hidden from human beings—the future—as well as what is hidden in them, in their consciousness (342). The seer understands the future through the ideal eternal pattern he discerns through considering the past; through considering the pattern of the temporal interaction of those things which are in humankind. The seer converts the certains of the past, which are hidden in the consciousness of humanity (that is, in the modifications of the human mind), and observes the unmade pattern of development that results. To do so is to experience the thunder of history.

History—the eternal pattern of human cose in their temporal passage—is not made by humanity, just as the thunder was not made by the first humans. The thunder was an external necessity that drove them to create the master image of Jove in order to confer intelligibility upon what they had witnessed. Verene notes that "the imaginative universal of Jove is an intelligibility or a true because it is made by the power of *fantasia*, but this first form of *scienza*, a *scienza in divinità*, imitates; that is, it is based on a *coscienza* of the divine, a witnessing awareness of the other."[29]

When we grasp that the human world always begins in necessity and always ends in madness, the necessity of the terror of the cycles of history crashes in on us as well, and we form the image of the ideal eternal history. We attempt to tell ourselves a fable in brief about the development of the civil world. Our learned ignorance is then an analogue to the simple ignorance of the first humans; in striving to become divine, we find that all we can do is end up pointing at it. But this pointing, this witnessing, becomes a basis for our imitation of the divine.

We did not make the thunder. We do not make the rise and fall of the nations. We do not will (or intend) that nations should rise into civil happiness through the agency of those very things that would seem to imply happiness' very opposite—the bestial lusts and vices that run throughout the human race (132). Nor do we will that the nations should decline into horror and madness through the very glories of human reason that would seem to imply the very opposite of decline (1106). So Vico notes that "out of ferocity, avarice, and ambition, the three vices which run throughout the human race, [legislation] creates the military, merchant, and governing classes, and thus the strength, riches, and wisdom of commonwealths. . . . This axiom proves there is divine providence and further that it is a divine legislative mind. For out of the passions of men[,] each bent on private advantage . . . it has made the civil institutions" (133). But then, when reason has reached its zenith, "providence decrees that . . . they shall turn their cities into forests and the forests into dens and lairs of men. In this way, through long centuries of barbarism, rust will consume the misbegotten subtleties of malicious wits that have turned them into beasts made more inhuman by the barbarism of reflection than the first men had been made by the barbarism of sense" (1106).

This means, as Verene notes, that "history is an activity of the production of illusion, but the production of the opposite of truth is itself a truth. This is the truth that there is a providence in history. The ideal eternal history once grasped in *fantasia* places us in a position to understand the specific nature of this process."[30] The heroic movement of thought that the seer then attempts is an effort to grasp the connection of the oppositions in history in light of the divine pattern, and heroic thought is the thought of unresolved opposition grasped in a truly learned ignorance.[31]

Scienza of things human then rests upon coscienza of things divine. Both together make up wisdom, which is a prudential and jurisprudential self-knowledge based upon memory. Vico rejects the optimism of the new mathematical sciences because they lack self-knowledge. They do not know who they are or what it means to be human.

Reform or Self-knowledge?

A conceptually based theory, and the method it embodies, is essentially comic in its optimism. In rejecting memory, such a theory also neglects the narrative of beginning and end, resulting in a plotless comedy of logic. Descartes's *Discourse* can serve as an emblem of this.[32]

Vico writes in his *Autobiography:* "We shall not here feign what René Descartes craftily feigned as to the method of his studies simply in order to exalt his own philosophy and mathematics and degrade all the other studies included in divine and human erudition. Rather, with the candor proper to a historian, we shall narrate plainly and step by step the entire series of Vico's studies, in order that the proper and natural causes of his particular development as a man of letters may be known" (*A* 113/5). Here Vico notes that the central concern of Descartes's account of his method is not a history but a theoretical aim, which structures the account he gives.[33]

Descartes notes in the *Discourse* that "in this discourse I shall be happy to show the paths I have followed, and to set forth my life as in a picture [*tableau*]."[34] Verene notes that Descartes's choice of *tableau* to refer to his account of his life is apropos, given the major image that dominates the work: "himself, as the I, the subject, the thinker in the tableau of the stove-heated room."[35]

Descartes centers his work on the static self-portrait of the solitary I, in its stove-heated room, who disowns the ancient cities of memory in favor of a new metropolis that will "conform to the unity of a rational scheme."[36] He feigns that he is the "I" of Everyman, epitomizing "the power of forming a good judgment and of distinguishing the true from the false, which is properly speaking what is called Good Sense or Reason, [and] is by nature equal in all men."[37]

This "I" of *le bon sens* has no historical causes, and the thoughts it thinks no real antecedents. Indeed, Descartes deliberately states, or as Vico has it, craftily feigns, that the opposite is the case—that the good sense he found in himself had nothing to do with what he had achieved in completing "the entire course of study at the close of which one is usually received into the ranks of the learned."[38]

So Descartes discounts as causes for the "I" of good sense, one by one, languages, literature, history, philosophy, science, jurisprudence, and rhetoric, in an antinarrative of reductive apotheosis.[39] Only mathematics receives praise, but it has been ignored and misused! Everything points to the static tableau of the solitary "I," sitting in a room with his thoughts, discovering his four-step inertial guidance system.

To proceed under the aegis of an inertial guidance system is to be supremely detached from one's surroundings and independent of its influences. Such a detachment essentially involves a sense of the comic. Hartle has pointed out the importance of the motif of the absence of human connection and the resulting implication of the category of the comic to an understanding of Descartes's work. She emphasizes Descartes's statement in the third part of the *Discourse* that in the nine years following his discovery of the method, "I did nought but roam hither and thither, trying to be a spectator rather than an actor in all the comedies the world displays."[40]

The comedies Descartes witnesses consist in a deviation from the standard of knowledge that he had discovered in the heated room. Hartle notes that "from the standpoint of 'certain knowledge' it is variable custom itself that can appear laughable, especially when it takes itself seriously. Descartes in his travels is the spectator of custom and from this standpoint all customs are equal. None is ridiculous in relation to any other, and all are laughable in relation to certain knowledge."[41]

Descartes seeks to mask himself as a participant in the comedy; the first maxim of his provisional morality is to blend in with local custom and morality in order to hide his stance as a spectator. Hartle notes that this masked detachment allows the confusions, errors, and uncertainty he observes to appear comic: "There is no comparable mention of tragedy in the *Discourse*, and nothing is even described as pitiable. What comes closest is the mention of 'sadness' as one among the 'imperfections' not found in God and from which Descartes would willingly be free. . . . There is no mention of any tragic error in the *Discourse* as a whole or in connection with Descartes' own life."[42]

The detachment of the spectator, of the one who merely witnesses and reflects upon the world, is essential to the modern geometrical method. In ignoring memory and the historical reality of the things that are its province, everything becomes simple, disconnected, and analyzable into atemporal parts. A good example of this is the piece of wax Descartes considers in his *Meditations*. In "Meditation II" it becomes for a detached intellectual vision merely extension precisely because memory is suppressed: "What did I know distinctly in this piece of wax? . . . Perhaps it was what I now think, viz., that this wax was not that sweetness of honey, nor that agreeable scent of flowers, nor that particular whiteness, nor that figure, nor that sound, but simply a body which a little while before appeared to me as perceptible under these forms, and which is now perceptible under others."[43]

Descartes's wax has no plot, no memory structure. It has neither beginning nor end but only a deviation from the standards of perfect knowing, a deviation that Descartes optimistically knows he can overcome. The memory and history of the wax only confuse the issue and comically complicate a real knowledge of it, as did the men Descartes encountered in his travels. Indeed, he explicitly compares the wax with men: "When looking from a window and saying I see men who pass in the street, I really do not see them, but infer that what I see is men, just as I say that I see the wax. And yet what do I see from the window but hats and coats which may cover automatic machines?"[44] The world of human beings, considered apart from imagination and memory, becomes a comic automated puppet show. Without the tether and tang of the particular, it is reduced to the spectacle of a Cartesian Punch and Judy extravaganza.[45] Verene notes that "there is no tragedy in the logical comprehension of an event, because it has no plot. Logic is comic. The logical concept never faces the aspect of events that makes them tragic because it never participates in memory."[46]

At most, Descartes can be uncertain, held in suspense, waiting to resume the progressive march the method guarantees us. He can make a clean sweep of the errors of the past, for the archai for him are not governing roots but only another set of detached simples to be factored into the equation. An origin for a spectator is an object of reflection. Reflection, as Verene notes, is a fascination with objects that are external to the knower and not essentially tied to his own existence.[47]

But speculation is rooted in memory. It does not seek to witness the world as a spectator but to engage its governing roots in an attempt at self-knowledge. It imitates the origin, seeking to remake it as something true in the present, seeking to frame a fable in brief of the self's temporal journey through the world and the paths it has taken to reach its current standpoint. Human beings seen in the street through the window are not mere static simples viewed as disconnected shapes; they possess the continuity of past interactions that guarantee through memory and imagination that they are humans, not machines. And any speculative account of a piece of wax will always include its past association with flowers, bees, and honey because speculation takes the whole as its object.

Such an account is historical, temporal—the very opposite of Descartes's tableau of static simples. Speculation must make use of all the elements of the cultural world that Descartes rejected, for they are the topical storehouses from which can be drawn the material necessary for the construction of a narrative. The story of the individual philosopher is, then, a microcosm, organically related to the macrocosm of humanity. Verene notes that the philosopher's "own sense of self-knowledge, the narrative or potential narrative of his self, must be accomplished in terms of the same principles whereby the life of the collective is understood. For the philosopher of history, in Vico's terms, the Greek polis becomes all of history or, as Vico puts it in Augustinian terms, 'that great city of the human race.'"[48]

Self-knowledge denies the possibility of endless comic reform precisely because it operates in terms of the reality of the archai that governs the development of all the human cose. The central reality of this for the Vichian new scientist is the knowledge of his or her own temporal location in the pattern of human development: the time of the third age.

This fact gives the speculative knower the endlessly negative task of attempting to bring the origins into the present in the only way possible for a third age thinker—as something that is "intelligibly poetic."[49] We attempt to remake the origin in a speech of the whole. But "thought cannot actually make the world as true as it can in the life of poetic wisdom. It can bring the origin into the present but in doing so it is driven by the very age of which it is a part to make the origin intelligible."[50] But at least we know who we are and what it means to be human.

An Unorthodox Science

In Chapter 5 I noted that to one who was familiar with the commonplace tradition, many aspects of Vico's thought would become evident that might otherwise remain hidden. The obverse of this is true as well: to one unversed in the commonplace tradition, much may forever remain unclear about Vico's new science. The work of Attila Fáj and Leon Pompa on Vico's axioms is a case in point. As Fáj, in particular, is the only person to have written in detail on Vico's axioms, it is important to see where he and I both agree and disagree. Pompa approaches Vico in terms of his theory of knowledge, so it is important to see how his account differs from mine as well.

Fáj points to the *Institutes* and the *Study Methods* as key texts for understanding Vico's scientific method.[51] Focusing on these texts, he claims that in Vico the epicheireme is "the perfect method used by eloquent rhetors, as well as by extremely careful scientific researchers, when they discuss questions about nature, man, and state from antithetical viewpoints."[52] Fáj then identifies a Vichian axiom with an enthymemic sentence.[53] Fáj here identifies the epicheireme, or dialectical syllogism, with the enthymeme, in the manner of traditional Aristotelian scholarship. As should be evident from my discussion in Chapter 6, such an identification strikes me as mistaken.

The traditional view, of course, is that an enthymeme is the purely logical "mutilated syllogism" of Cartesian Port-Royal logic. Following William J. Grimaldi, I claimed in Chapter 6 that an enthymeme is the instrument of an organic discourse that takes into account the whole speech situation of orator and audience. Fáj, on the other hand, identifies the epicheireme with the enthymeme and then the enthymeme qua epicheireme with a Vichian axiom. Fáj writes that Vico "removes the contrast between the *loci dialectici* and the *loci rhetorici*."[54] On the contrary, Vico sharpens that distinction, before descending through it to achieve something new. It is this novelty that makes his enthymeme so hard to recognize.

For Fáj the Vichian axiom qua epicheireme offers a new and better method of scientific discovery that anticipates much of the new thinking on the logic of science in our own century. Vico's methodology is progressive, allowing him to anticipate novel modern sciences such as "acoustical biology," which establishes how the acoustical phenomena of living organisms "fulfill the function of communication in the life of living beings and examines the prerequisites, conditions, and contents of such communication."[55]

Vico anticipated this discipline through showing in his science how the first humans transferred the sound of the thunder into a language of mute gestures out of the necessity of their lack of speech. His epicheiremic logic enabled him to anticipate the results of a ground-breaking modern discipline like bio-acoustics. According to Fáj, he should not, then, be viewed as merely eccentric but as a man ahead of his time; indeed, far ahead of Descartes, whose logic was less progressive, and who was thus unable to anticipate novel sciences.[56] Vico was also a better Cartesian than Descartes in that he noted the applicability of science to the social world, anticipating the modern social sciences.

So for Fáj, Vico corrects the mistakes of methodology in the Cartesian program through an unorthodox logic of scientific discovery. He tinkers with the machinery of scientific methodology but makes no attempt to alter its basic progressive purpose. For Fáj, Vico's *logic* is unorthodox, but his *science* is not; it seems strange to us only because of its visionary status. Citing recent advances in understanding the logic of contemporary scientific research, Fáj writes that "these and other trends of contemporary logic follow, in different ways and more or less consciously, the line drawn by the Neapolitan philosopher."[57]

In this way topical thinking is made a subspecies of logic, just as it was in the tradition of the late Renaissance—a tradition through which Vico had to descend in order to recover an authentic Aristotelian rhetoric. Vico looks back to topical thinking in the Renaissance only to look back farther still—not farther ahead. Vico thinks the origin. And what he offers is not an unorthodox logic of scientific discovery but an unorthodox science of logical discovery. His scienza redefines the logos and offers a new standard of logic and discovery through the maker's imagination, giving the notion of a "logical proof" an entirely different sense from that of a new and improved method of scientific discovery.

It might seem natural at this point to consider the Pompa's work on the epistemology, logic, and methodology of the *New Science*.[58] But Pompa unfortunately nowhere considers the status of Vico's axioms qua axioms in his account of the "theory of knowledge" in the *New Science*. He does not define what he thinks an axiom is as such or what it means in the *Scienza nuova*. He seems to assume that we all know what an axiom is and that Vico's understanding of an axiom is the same as ours.

What does an axiom mean? What might it mean for Vico? As Vico notes, "Doctrines must take their beginnings from the matters of which they treat" (314). The axiomatics of a system are the key to the structuring principles of that system, and to ignore the question of what an axiom is seems curious.

In addition, Pompa's explicit rejection of what he calls the humanist interpretation, to include the interpretations of Isaiah Berlin, B. A. Haddock, and Donald Phillip Verene, further precludes his recognition of the topical character of Vico's thinking.[59] The sections in which Pompa claims to examine topical thinking (pp. 186, 190–195, 231) make no reference to topical method in the classical or the Renaissance tradition, merely offering a cursory summary of Vico's account of topics in *Study Methods* and *Ancient Wisdom*. Like Descartes, Pompa seems intent on discounting the value of reading ancient authors.

Here we see that Max Fisch was right in his statement that Pompa "likes to avoid the technicalities of Vico's time and substitute technicalities of our own."[60] Fáj's analysis is more subtle and careful than Pompa's, but Fáj ultimately finds himself at one with Pompa's belief that although Vico's thought represents a "highly unusual sort of science," it is nonetheless a science of the modern type.[61] Both men place Vico in a rationalistic framework. And although Fáj does seek to engage the technicalities of Vico's time, his rationalistic framework does not seem to allow him to get them quite right.

The central disagreement I have with both analyses is their apparent failure to recognize the central imperative of self-knowledge in the *Scienza nuova*, which makes it a book of wisdom rather than a manual of scientific discovery and reform. These accounts miss the irony of Vico's calling his new way of knowing a science, because they downplay the topical tradition in which he writes; and the analyses fail to sense the even more subtle irony of Vico's employing geometric nomenclature in the exposition of his "new science." Vico's science, then, becomes one of reform in the service of an optimistic program of scientific progress. Vico wishes instead to examine the things of human making in terms of their origin in a particular time and place, viewing them as well in terms of their inevitable decline and fall. Every birth forecasts its own death. As Vico notes: "Men first feel necessity, then look for utility, next attend to comfort, still later amuse themselves with pleasure, thence grow dissolute in luxury, and finally go mad and waste their substance" (241).

8 What Is Worth Thinking?

In introducing section II of Book I of the *Scienza nuova*, "Degli elementi" (Of the elements), Vico states: "Per dar forma adunque alle materie qui innanzi apparecchiate sulla Tavola cronologica, proponiamo ora qui i seguenti assiomi o degnità così filosofiche come filologiche, alcune poche, ragionevoli e discrete domande, con alquante schiarite diffinizioni; le quali, come per lo corpo animato il sangue, così deono per entro scorrervi ed animarla in tutto ciò questa Scienza ragiona della comune natura delle nazioni [In order to give form to the materials set in order herebefore in the Chronological Table, we now propose the following axioms or 'thoughts worth thinking,' both philosophical and philological, some few, reasonable and proper postulates, with some clarified definitions, which, as the blood flows through animate bodies, so will they within this science and animate it in all its reasonings about the common nature of the nations]" (119).

Here I offer a more literal translation of the entire passage than do T. G. Bergin and M. H. Fisch in order to make clear a distinction that their translation obscures. For the phrase "pronomio ora qui i seguenti assiomi o degnità," Bergin and Fisch offer "we now propose the following axioms." Their translation collapses the two terms *assiomi* and *degnità* into one.

But Vico specifically says "assiomi o degnità," and in all the 114 passages that follow he consistently refers to his *elementi* as *degnità*. In a corollary to his first degnità, for example, he states: "Questa degnità è la cagione di que'due comuni costumi umani [This 'axiom' is the cause of those two human customs]" (121). The usage is similar in his other elementi.

Vico first calls his "elements" *assiomi o degnità*, and then uniformly refers to them as *degnità*. What are we to make of this?

The Authority of Philology

Bruno Migliorini, in *The Italian Language*, points to Vico's espousal of Tuscanism to explain the way he uses terms. Tuscanism was a movement that promoted the idea of basing written Italian on the dialect of Trecento Tuscany. It particularly affected writing in vocabulary, which involved the use of archaisms from the Duecento and Trecento, and in syntax, which involved frequent inversions and complexity of style.[1]

In southern Italy the pro-Tuscan movement began at the school of Lionardo di Capua (1617–1695) in Naples. In the *Autobiography*, Vico praised "the most erudite Lionardo di Capua," who "had restored good Tuscan prose, and cultivated it with grace and beauty" (*A* 133/17). Vico further identifies himself as "a friend of those men of letters who had been partisans of di Capua" (*A* 148/25) and explains that in his writing he wished to "try how well the delicate sensibility of the Greeks could be united with the grandeur of Latin expression, and how much of both the Italian tongue could combine" (*A* 181/43). And finally, he states that "his youthful study of good writers in the vulgar tongue . . . enabled him in his old age . . . to make splendid use of that tongue in composing the *New Science*" (*A* 178/42).

So Migliorini writes that Vico, himself "feeling the need to create a language of his own, turned not only to the Latins, but to Tuscan words belonging to the 'heroic' age of the language. In Vico's purism, we have . . . not just the purism of L. di Capua and N. Annenta, but the purism of a writer whose gaze rested on the past and who wished to preserve its voice in his pages."[2]

Vico's use of archaisms in his new science can be related to the explosion of scientific terminology in eighteenth-century Italy, which, as Migliorini notes, affected all aspects of life and culture. So "in fact writers of all kinds frequently had recourse to scientific terms for metaphors."[3] Migliorini adds in light of this that "Vico manifested his personal tastes not so much in creation of neologisms as in the choice of archaic and rare words (*degnità*, *eroe*, etc.)."[4]

According to the *Grande dizionario della lingua Italiana*, the first use of the word *degnità* as a "principio filosofico generale, di per sè evidente: assioma [general philosophical principle, which is of itself evident: axiom]," is by Giambattista Domenico Gelli of Florence.[5] Gelli was the famous shoemaker who became a luminary of the Florentine Academy.

Gelli was interested in the origins of both the Italian people and their language. He based his theories on etymological discoveries, claiming that Tuscany had been inhabited long before the time of Sulla and that the Italians were civilized long before the Greeks.[6] Armand De Gaetano writes that Gelli "further believed in cultural cycles which vaguely foreshadow Vico and maintains that when the civilization of a people has reached its peak it declines to its original state and then starts over again."[7] In support of his theories Gelli not only looked to linguistic investigations but also claimed as evidence "folklore material as well as remains of ancient structures. . . . He seems to believe, among other things, the reports about the bones of some giants who were supposed to have been over one hundred yards tall."[8] Gelli's work was popularized through his friend Pier Francesco Giumballari, who used Gelli as the spokesman in an extremely popular work called *Il Gello*, which repeated Gelli's ideas in a simpler format.[9] Vico cites *Il Gello* in axiom CII (305).[10]

Gelli advocated the replacement of the classical languages with the vernacular, in particular, Tuscan. This was a part of the educational program of the Florentine Academy, which in its famous *lezioni*, or public academic lectures, on science, philosophy, history, and the like, sought to popularize the arts and sciences.[11] A key element in the program was to find a good equivalent in the vernacular for a Latin or Greek technical term, in this way producing a new scientific language that avoided the obscurities of the *dotti*, the learned professors.[12] So for the Latin *axioma* we find substituted the Italian *degnità*.

The Latin *axioma* is a transliteration of the Greek, and it refers only to one sense of the Greek term, that of a principle or axiom.[13] The Italian *degnità* restores to the terminology all the connotations of the original Greek word. The word ἀξίωμα primarily involves the idea of worth or dignity. It is related to the verb ἀξιόω, which means "to think or deem worthy."[14] The word ἀξιόω also means "to think one worthy to do or be."[15] Thus, an ἀξίωμα was "that of which one is thought worthy, an honor."[16] In this way the word could also refer to an office, rank, or position held as an honor.

From these usages developed the sense of "that which is thought fit" by the holder of the position or office and became "a decree."[17] And finally it came to mean "that which is assumed as the basis of demonstration."[18] An ἀξίωμα is that which is thought fit, or deemed worthy, to stand as the archē, or beginning point and foundation, of the area of knowledge under consideration. So an ἀξίωμα is literally "a thought worth thinking."

In a parallel fashion, the Italian word *degnità* primarily involves the verb *degnare*, which means "to deem worthy, to regard as worthy."[19] From it is derived *degnità*, which signifies dignity, rank, or an office held in honor.[20] The *Grande dizionario* defines *degnità* as "condizione abituale e coerentemente perseguita . . . che nasce dalle qualità intrinseche e essenziali dell'uomo, e si fonda sul suo comportameto e sul suo contegno nei rapporti sociali sui propri meriti e sul proprio grado [a habitual condition, consistently pursued . . . that arises from the intrinsic and essential qualities of man and that is founded upon his deportment and bearing in a social context, in accordance with his appropriate merit and status]."[21] It is used in this sense by Dante, Cristoforo Landino, Francesco Guicciardini, Tasso, and Boccaccio (who are among the authors the Florentine Academy looked to in developing their vernacular language of science).

So the use of *degnità* for axiom calls to mind all the associations the word had in the original Greek because of its parallel status in the vernacular. It allows connotations to arise that *assioma*, the other Italian word for axiom, does not. *Assioma* is directly derived form the Latin *axioma*, and it is similarly restricted in its connotations to the notion of an axiom as a self-evident truth or principle.[22] But *degnità* has the rhetorical character of *proprietas*, in that it more fully signifies the complex meaning of its object.[23]

What is the *philosophical* significance of these *philological* considerations? What truth lies in the word *degnità* for the science of Vico?

The Reasons of Philosophy

Vico published his first *New Science* in October 1725. It was a recasting of an earlier *New Science* in negative form. This negative version was apparently an exposition of his views through a critical analysis of seventeenth-century natural-law theorists, as well as such thinkers as John Locke and Descartes.[24]

This no-longer-extant manuscript was apparently too large to publish, Vico having lost the financial support of Cardinal Lorenzo Corsini. So he rewrote the entire work in positive form, greatly reducing its size, and financed the work himself through the sale of a diamond ring. Thus appeared the *Principi di una scienza nuova intorno all'natura delle nazioni per la quale si ritruovano i principi di altro sistema del diritto naturale delle genti* (Principles of a new science concerning the nature of the nations, by which are found the principles of another system of the natural law of the gentes).[25]

By 1728 Vico was urged to publish a new edition of his work by Fr. Carlo Lodoli, censor of publications in Venice, who invited him to make corrections or additions as he wished. They were sent to Lodoli in October 1729, but the printer, Vico says, acted in ways that displeased him, and he insisted the manuscript be returned to him (*A* 183, 191–192/145, 53–54).

This work was again too long for any publisher to undertake, so Vico "hit upon a new plan which was perhaps best of all, though save for this necessity he would not have thought of it. By comparing [the text of the new edition] with that of the first edition, one may see how completely different it is. For everything that he had split up and dispersed in the Annotations to preserve the plan of the first edition . . . is now composed and ordered by a single spirit. By virtue of this consecutive order, which even more than propriety of style is a principle cause of brevity, the second edition exceeds by only six pages the first plus the manuscript [that was sent to Venice]" (*A* 192/45).

Vico claims here that necessity drove him to brevity. His trouble with the printer was, then, one of the occasions of fortune that philosophers "meditate" and that can point us to an understanding of Vico's intellectual life and how it resulted in the *New Science* (*A* 182/44). I shall now focus on the notion of brevity as an occasion of fortune and tie it in with Vico's use of geometric nomenclature. For if we compare the first with the second *New Science*, we are immediately struck by the greater compression of the second edition within parallel passages, as well as by the affectation of a geometric method. How can we explain this?

The biographer H. P. Adams notes that the first *New Science* was neither well received nor understood—indeed, only a few men, like Lodoli, Count Gian Artico di Porcìa, or Abbé Antonio Conti, noticed it at all. Adams comments that "nothing irritated Vico more than to hear that the work was obscure."[26] But Vico also "understood that the age of Descartes and Locke was not propitious to his own work."[27] It was the age of the new method, which neglected the human for the mathematical studies and which misunderstood the function of ingenium in discovering truth.[28]

But the occasions of fortune were driving Vico to condense his work and make it more "pointed." Recall Vico's statement in the *Autobiography* that he wrote the account of his life "as a philosopher, meditating the causes, natural and moral, and the occasions of fortune . . . which were destined later to bear fruit in those reflections on which he built his final work, the *New Science*, which was to demonstrate that his intellectual life was bound to have been such as it was and not otherwise" (*A* 182/44).

Vico tells us in his *Autobiography* how Jean Le Clerc had written to him of his *Universal Law* that it "was 'full of recondite matters condensed from various points of view, and written in a very compact style,' which meant that it was constructed by 'mathematical method,' which 'from few principles draws infinite consequences'" (*A* 164/34). Here we see brevity and "mathematical method" conjoined in Vico's mind through another occasion of fortune.

Mario Fubini has cited brevity as one of the essential stylistic differences between the first and second *New Science*s. Fubini connects this change with Vico's tendency toward the aphoristic style of the humanists. Vico's necessity to condense his work happily coincided with his tendency to write in a concise and epigrammatic manner.[29] And Fausto Nicolini points to "le più belle, brevi e famose degnità [the most beautiful, concise, and famous 'axioms']" as the prime example of Vico's "lapidarietà [lapidary style]."[30]

In my discussion in Chapter 5 of the topical style of Renaissance humanism, epitomized in the works of Baltasar Graciàn and Francis Bacon, among others, I noted that the common factor was precisely that condensation of meaning in epigrammatic style on which Vico began to concentrate in the second *New Science*. Christopher Maurer described that style as "antithesis and paradox; the constant use of ellipses; the concentration of meaning brought about by punning and other sorts of wordplay; the lack of connective tissue between one sentence—one point—and another (notice that there is often an abrupt transition between aphorism and commentary, and that the commentaries themselves often seem disjointed and fragmentary)."[31]

This description limns the second *New Science*. One might even paraphrase the last clause to read "notice that there is often an abrupt transition between *axiom* and *corollary,* and that the *corollaries* themselves often seem disjointed and fragmentary." The style of the second *New Science,* and particularly of the axiom section, is essentially gnomic in character, displaying all the characteristics of topical methodology.

If one were to lay the *Scienza nuova* open to the axiom section, for example, and then lay Bacon's *Novum organum* by its side, one would be hard put to distinguish between them on a surface examination. Each contains section after section of varying lengths (numbered sequentially with Roman numerals), as well as a confluence of materials in the accepted Renaissance aphoristic style, which had developed out of the commonplace tradition. The only difference is Vico's affectation of a geometric nomenclature. Vico calls his loci axioms, while Bacon calls his aphorisms.

Vico's first *New Science* is less aphoristic, more "analytic," as Adams puts it, and so less "compressed."[32] It is more discursive and wordy, without the abrupt transitions of the second edition. Adams notes this but favors the style of the earlier edition. He does not see that Vico, owing to the occasions of fortune, has become in the second *Scienza nuova* more topically oriented, more engaged with the humanistic style of writing and that to underline his return to the style of the commonplace tradition in his "new science," Vico calls his enthymemes and aphorisms assioma o degnità.

Style and terminology clash in the *Scienza nuova*. The two seem impossible to connect. Vico gives us a section of gnomic enthymemes, arranged according to a more dynamic sense of topical methodology derived from Aristotle, and he calls his enthymemes axioms and his methodology geometric. Who among his contemporaries had the wit to see his joke?

Vico's style is entirely dissimilar from the classical statements of geometric method found in Galileo and the other new sciences of mathematical mechanics: it proceeds nothing like Descartes's *Geometry,* and it breathes a spirit entirely different from Spinoza's *Ethics*. His affectation of geometrical method thus seems entirely perverse and grotesque to anyone accustomed to the new tradition of the *more geometrico*. It would make one want to react as did the Neapolitan nobleman, who, according to G. F. Finetti, reported that Vico was thought learned up to the time that he published his *New Science:* "Oh! By then he had become completely mad!"[33] Only a person trained in topics could possibly see what Vico was doing and grasp the point of connecting such diverse things as topics and geometry; only someone with ingenium would "get the point."

In the axiom section Vico speaks as a philosopher-rhetorician, and as a philosopher he employs the trope of irony, as any thinker in the third age must do. But he does not operate with any maliciousness in his irony; there is no intent to deceive. Instead, his irony takes us back to the imaginative universal of philosophy in the West—the figure of Socrates. Gregory Vlastos identifies Vico's kind of irony as arising from Socrates and as being what Vlastos calls complex. According to Vlastos, "In complex irony what is said both is and isn't what is meant: its surface content is meant to be true in one sense, false in another."[34]

So not only does Vico say one thing and mean another in his use of geometric nomenclature—say axiom and mean gnomic enthymeme: say geometric and mean topical. He also means to mock the pretensions of Cartesian science in pointing to a realm where he thinks a real scienza can be found: the world of human things.

Is Vico serious in his use of axioms? Well, no, not as a literal-minded thinker might be. He is concerned with things so important that it would be impious to be serious about them. Vico is aware, as any philosopher must be, that to think one can speak straightforwardly about the realm of probabilities in which we live is one of the greatest of the conceits of scholars. So as a philosopher, he speaks under the trope of irony: the joke of a philosopher often has more import than the most elaborate considerations of a literal-minded thinker. Eloquence is never straightforward, for it is concerned with prudence.

The use of geometric nomenclature underlines the vigorous union of universal and particular—the certain and the true—in the enthymeme and points to the realm in which real truth—and thus real knowledge—can be found for Vico. Galileo's new science sought to geometricize nature, attempting, in Vico's opinion, to apply human truth (which was made) to a realm to which it could not apply, the world that only God could know, because God made it. Geometric nomenclature does not indicate the route to the authentic voice of the natural world, as the "new mechanics" had thought, but seems to be more properly applied to the world of human nature. Vico steals the terminology of the new mechanics to emphasize his insight. It is a witty conceit.

Vico thought that the thing all the new scientists had been seeking in the natural world was not there; necessity lay instead in self-knowledge through a maker's knowledge of the human world. That is where "thoughts worth thinking" are really to be found. The primary signification of *assioma* in the new sciences of Vico's time was the application of geometry to physical space, with an accompanying claim to necessity in its applications.

But this, Vico tells us, is not how one finds a degnità, a thought worth thinking. The natural world with reference to human knowers must be reckoned or esteemed something less than the realm of scienza. What is really worth thinking about is the world made by human beings; it is there we shall find our demonstrations and our axioms.

Thoughts worth thinking are to be found in the elements of the human world, which we then esteem as basic principles necessary for self-knowledge. Verene notes that "the search for truth has classically always placed the human in relation to something beyond the reach of any method or form of self-contained, step-by-step thinking and analyzing. The self's search for truth has commonly prized *ingenium* (the perception of connections among what otherwise seem separate) over method."[35]

Vico engages ingenium through his topical methodology, epitomized in his use of gnomic enthymemes as axioms. Vico writes that his axioms are principles of formation: "In order to give form to the materials . . . we now propose the following axioms or 'thoughts worth thinking' . . . which, as the blood flows through animate bodies, so will they within this science and animate it" (119).

Vico proposes an organic form of thought, modeled upon the form and organization of the body. We are not to deduce or parse out clear and certain chains of deduction with Vico's elements, for in this case, as the old saying has it, analysis is well—as death is well. In Cartesian thought we murder to dissect, guiding our surgery by clear and distinct axioms, draining the body of its blood in a misguided attempt to delimit our monstrous creation.

Instead, Vico wishes us to meditate on his axioms in their organic context; to narrate to ourselves the great truths of the body of human culture in an attempt to find for ourselves that wisdom it is proper and dignified for a human being to have: to find in this way degnità.

The Theaters of Memory

Ultimately what we face in metaphysics are words. Words can be understood in their relation to Vico's new science through a consideration of the Greek word *sēma*. The primary meaning of *sēma* is "a sign, mark, or token."[36] But it can also mean "a sign from heaven, omen, portent," as well as "a sign by which a grave is known, mound, cairn, barrow."[37] A sēma is a sign from the dead to the living, as well as an omen or portent.

As I stated previously, a "new scientist" is a seer who is involved with divination, which according to Vico is the ability to "understand what is hidden from men—the future—or what is hidden in them—their consciousness" (342). And hidden in the consciousness of men, in the modifications of the human mind, are signs from the dead to the living.

The first seers, Vico tells us, were watchers of the heavens "for the purposes of taking the auspices" (739). He adds that what they contemplated "were the first *mathēmata*, the first *theōrēmata*, the first sublime or divine things contemplated and observed by the nations" (739). In this way astronomy and astrology arose, and "both names signified divination, even as from the aforesaid theorems came the term theology for the science of the language of the gods in their oracles, auspices, and auguries. Thence finally mathematics descended to measure the earth" (739).

Through an exploration of human things, Vico's new science contemplates, with a mathematics descended to earth, the path of providence. "Philosophy undertakes to examine philology" and comes down to earth to examine the signs (sēmata)—which consist in "all histories of the languages, customs, and deeds of peoples in war and peace"—and "reduces it to the form of a science" (7).

Giuseppe Mazzotta notes that what Vico is talking about here should not be confused with the seventeenth-century science known as antiquarianism, which involved "the cult of ruins as the *disjecta membra* of a lost past."[38] Vico explicitly contrasted his approach with that of contemporary antiquarians through his idea that "the genuine beginning of knowledge is articulated by texts which are simultaneously poetic and theological."[39] The sēmata are signs from the dead *makers* of the past human world.

But we are not like the seers of the first humans, who contemplated a world filled with gods. As new seers, we are constrained to operate within the limits of intelligibility in the *corso* of the third age, and we gaze at the sēmata of the first humans precisely as signs. Mazzotta notes that in the discontinuity between poetic knowledge and reflective knowledge we find a gap in which Vico's science is located: "In this gap lie scattered and buried ciphers, inscriptions, devices, etymologies, fragmented texts. . . . This gap is man himself, *homo*, whose etymology from *humo* and *humando* . . . defines the burial ground as man's essence. But there is always an excess and a residue to the finite, partial entity called 'man,' for death, which divides the self from others, transforms individual projects into an object for other projects by other men."[40]

This means that the *Scienza nuova* does not give us Cartesian simples, disconnected shapes out of the past with which to form schematic wholes. As a work ruled by speculation, we have instead, as Mazzotta puts it, "a cultural and poetic rethinking of histories, memories, and shadows," which is accordingly written "in the mixed mode of brief essays, maxims, fables, and sentences."[41] This style gives us a poetic philosophy of history, a "mixture of lapidary fulgurations, oracular obscurities, and criticism that together reach toward a time when a new Homer, the true educator of Hellas and the blind seer of the past, will wage a mighty war against time and thereby reacquaint man with death's pageants."[42]

When as "new seers" we contemplate death's pageants, we find the *given*, the archai, with which metaphysics always starts. Death's pageants come before us in what is given to us in memory. Memory, in Vico's sense, involves the meditation of the beginning points of the human world, which I discussed in Chapter 3: the imaginative universals that as sensory topics were the means by which the human world was made. Metaphysics descends through memory to contemplate these beginnings.

Metaphysics begins and ends with words. Vico states that his "new science or metaphysics" (31), in considering the three ages of the world, finds "three kinds of languages"—of gods, heroes, and humans—that "compose the vocabulary of this science" (32). He adds: "We find that the principle of these origins both of languages and of letters lies in the fact that the first gentile peoples, by a demonstrated necessity of nature, were poets who spoke in poetic characters" (34).

We catch a glimpse of these beginning points or primary images in their remains in the languages of men; they are dim intimations colored by, as Mazzotta has it, "the thick shadows of the night, the tumults of the body, the fits of passion, man's dark and incandescent imaginings in the face of nature's perturbations, the 'mental dictionary' of history."[43] This is preeminently the realm of words, which operate in the realm of "interrelationships of distant echoes which can never be constituted into a unified totality."[44] As names that dimly signify their beginnings, words are "kept in their plural, irreducible dispersion, and the perimeter of their displacement is marked by their own law of the phonetic-semantic.[45] A metaphysics that begins and ends with words understands along with Johann Georg Hamann that "Deutlichkeit ist die richtige Vertheilung von Licht und Schatten."[46] In the light and the shadows of the indefinite nature of the human mind, the metaphysician confronts the signs from the dead to the living, which give us death's pageants in a theater of memory.

As Verene notes, Bacon had characterized philosophical systems as stage plays in philosophical theaters. These theaters, like the theaters of the poets, give us stories more unreal than the true stories of history, and for this reason they are for Bacon less worthy of respect. According to Verene, "Bacon comes close to stating an important truth, but his empirical conception of thought leads him away from it at just the moment he gives it birth as his fourth idol."[47]

It is precisely Vico's rejection of Bacon's fixation on the world of nature, of which we can only be certain, that leads him to a deeper insight. Mazzotta, commenting on the difference between Vico's and Bacon's tree of knowledge, states that "the idea that knowledge is historical . . . is grafted by Vico, in a radical departure from Bacon's myth of knowledge as rooted in nature, onto the notion that history is coextensive with poetry."[48]

This brings to mind Aristotle's distinction in the *Poetics* between poetry and history. There, Aristotle writes that "the poet and the historian are not distinguished because one speaks metrically and the other ametrically; . . . but this distinguishes them: one tells what happened, and the other what might happen."[49] This is the part Bacon understands. But Aristotle goes on to add: "On account of this poetry is more philosophical and noble than history; for poetry speaks the universal much more, while history speaks according to the particular."[50]

When philosophy undertook to examine philology, it found that the beginnings of history were made by the poets as originary makers. Metaphysics thus arises, as Verene notes, "not out of a new look at physical nature but out of a new sense of ordering what is already ordered in the myth. . . . The myth makes the original truths of thought. In the myth the power of the word is first realized."[51] When philosophy examines philology, it "recreates the essentials of the world in language."[52] The world is then remade into a maker's knowledge that consists in linguistic expressions—a "theater of words."[53]

In Chapter 5 I discussed the memory systems of the Renaissance and suggested that Vico's *Scienza nuova* could be understood through them. I now wish to explain Vico's theater of memory through a reconsideration of the memory tradition of the Renaissance—and in particular, the memory system of Giulio Camillo, which in many ways summed up the art of memory in the Renaissance.[54]

The memory systems of the Renaissance grafted the principle of the microcosm onto classical roots. An orator would speak not only from his particular perspective but also with the dignity appropriate to human nature "from a memory organically affiliated to the proportions of the divine harmony."[55] It was the "divine Camillo," as his contemporaries called him, who first fully understood the implications of this.

Giulio Camillo Delmino was, as Frances Yates notes, one of the most famous men of the sixteenth century—though little known today.[56] Born in 1480, he was at one time a professor of dialectics at Bologna, but he spent most of his life working on a memory system that he called a *Theatro della memoria*.[57] What we know of the theater comes from Camillo's *L'Idea del theatro*, dictated on seven mornings in 1544, shortly before his death.[58]

We may take the famous Theater of Memory as an emblem, as it were, of the elements of the Renaissance world that will enable us to understand the *Scienza nuova* as a memory system. The key move Camillo made was to transfer the mental and visual spaces of the artificial memory as found in the commonplace and emblem books into an actual architectural space. As Marco Frascari notes, "his aim was to develop a memory system that could embody the entire universe of human thought in an edifice/machine. This was a *fabbrica*, i.e., a theater where the mnemonic power of topical images would activate imagination and inspiration."[59] A mock-up of this three-dimensional commonplace book was seen by Vigilius Zuichemus, a secretary to Erasmus. Zuichemus, in a letter to Erasmus, quotes Camillo as saying that the structure was "a built or a constructed mind or soul."[60]

Zuichemus further reports that Camillo "pretends that all things that the human mind can conceive and which we cannot see with the corporeal eye, after being collected together by diligent meditation may be expressed by certain corporeal signs in such a way that the beholder may at once perceive with his eyes everything that is otherwise hidden in the depths of the human mind. And it is because of this corporeal looking that he calls it a theater."[61] The theater rose in seven grades or steps, divided by seven gangways, which represented the seven planets. On each of the gangways were seven gates, decorated with images. Wenneker Lu Beery notes that "from images chosen from everyday life, people and places that one knew, he moved to images chosen from mythology, the Cabala, and Hermetic literature."[62] Camillo's theater was composed of divine and human images that were thought, through memory, to unlock the secrets of the universe.

In this unusual theater there is only one spectator, who, in an inversion of the normal theater, stands where the stage would be, observing the elaborate series of emblems on the seven times seven gates where the audience would usually be; the emblems were then conjoined with drawers containing various written texts.[63] Here, too, res and verba combine.

In his study of Camillo's theater, Beery notes that the idea of the microcosm dominated Camillo's mind during his work on the theater. He would sometimes write of his *fabbrica* as a human body, which was a traditional motif for the microcosm. Frascari notes that "Camillo's basic idea, and the obsession of his life, was to organize an encyclopedia of human knowledge arranged like a human body within the analogous structure of theater, a small scale *imago mundi* embodied in an *imago corpori.*"[64]

Writing to Marc Antonio Flamino, Camillo calls his memory system, understood as a microcosm, a "meravigliosa fabbrica del corpo humano [a marvelous construction of the human body]."[65] In another place he refers to his memory system as a reverse anatomy: instead of exposing the framework of the body, he will reclothe it with ideas, on seven levels. Here we see the images of body, microcosm, and theater fused.[66] Camillo's theater, Frascari notes, "represented an anatomical projection of the construction of human memory, a corporeal tool for topical imagining."[67]

Camillo writes that the labor of his theater is to "find an order . . . which will keep the mind awake and move the memory."[68] His theater is a system of memory on a grand scale—an emblem book in three dimensions, sprung to life. According to Camillo, "This high and incomparable placing not only performs the office for conserving for us things, words, and arts which we need to confide to it, so that we may find them at once whenever we need them, but also gives us true wisdom from whose founts we come to the knowledge of things from their causes and not from their effects."[69] Here, as Verene notes, "the art of memory becomes the art of metaphysics."[70]

Camillo's metaphysics was founded in the image, not the concept. It was a metaphysics compatible with human frailty—consonant with human beings' inevitable ties to the image in their thinking. Curiously enough, this then becomes the route to the divine. Verene notes that "the theater is a placement of the world's places that exists within the world. The relationship between divine place and human place is an indeterminate relationship. It is closed to logic and open to the image. The essence of the image is to hold together indeterminately. Metaphysics must be an art of images or else it will remain a strictly human art."[71] Only through the indefinite nature of the human mind can we find a way to the intimations of the divine.

Camillo also called his Theatro della memoria a *Theatro della sapienza*.[72] With Camillo's Theater of Wisdom the complex Renaissance cultural artifact known as the artificial memory reached its apotheosis. It became for his contemporaries the perfect expression of, as Yates puts it, "the idea of a memory organically geared to the universe."[73] The divine Camillo and his theater haunted the intellectual consciousness of his age, and the memory of it lasted well into the eighteenth century.[74]

In Vico's theater there are both words and images, just as in Camillo's, the work being dominated by the dipintura that serves as frontispiece to his text. The *Scienza nuova* is a type of emblem book, then, with the image at the front needing to be consulted, as Vico states, both before and after reading the work (1).[75]

We saw in Chapter 5 how the emblem book complicates the relation between reader and text, making the reader a self-conscious spectator of the drama that a verbal-visual interaction creates. Recall from Charles Mosley that the emblem book became in this way a *theatrum mundi* and a fable in brief. Vico states at the end of his commentary on the picture that "we may now recapitulate all the prime elements of this world of nations by reference to the hieroglyphs that stand for them" (40).

The "prime elements of this world of nations" is precisely the *lingua mentale comune* that embodies the vocabulary of Vico's science (32, 161–162). As I stated previously, these elements are rooted in the sensus communis, the common sense of the human race. We remember Vico's statement that "common sense is judgement without reflection, shared by an entire class, an entire people, an entire nation, or the entire human race" (142).[76] When the "founders of humanity applied themselves to a sensory topics" (495), they created this common language in hewing out the sensory topics and "inventing" the commonplaces that make up the primary elements of orientation in the midst of the original flux (497). Original knowledge, then, concerns a metaphysics of the body and a logic of the senses (see Chapter 3, above).

Verene notes that "each nation must realize its mother tongue as a particular version of this common mental language. Every language is a memory system for recalling this language of original commonplaces, which is the unwritten and unspoken language beneath any language."[77] Vico's science uses recollective fantasia, a metaphysical art of memoria, to descend to the roots of the world. Vico's anabasis essentially involves the art of memory. And it is a metaphysics that begins and ends with the image, a method that is compatible with human frailty.

The Elements

In Vico's theater, the degnità, along with the omnipresent frontispiece, take the place of the images and the text in Camillo's theater.[78] Vico states that his elementi will flow through his science like blood through a body, animating it (119). He explicitly uses the image of the body here, fusing it with the idea of his fabbrica, just as Camillo does in calling to mind the principle of the microcosm when he refers to his memory system a marvelous fabbrica of the human body. And just as the first men understood all things through the simple ignorance of bodily metaphysics, so will the seers of the third age achieve metaphysics through a learned ignorance of bodily thought.

In keeping with the complexity of an emblem book, the parts of Vico's book are also represented in the symbolic frontispiece; macrocosm and microcosm are both symbolically present in the microcosm itself. Vico states that "the whole idea of this work may be summed up as follows. The darkness in the background is the material of this Science, uncertain, unformed, obscure, which is set forth in the Chronological Table. . . . The ray with which divine providence lights up the breast of metaphysic represents the axioms, definitions, and postulates that this Science takes as elements from which to deduce the principles on which it is based and the method by which it proceeds. All these things are contained in the first book" (41).

In the microcosmic body of the *Scienza nuova*, the elementi, represented as a ray and found in the axiom section of the book, lights up metaphysic, and then darts across the unformed material of the world of nations, which is represented in the microcosm of the book in the chronological table. Recall that Vico stated that he proposed his axioms in order to give form to this material (119).

Vico further states that the ray which represents the elementi strikes a convex jewel on the breast of Lady Metaphysic. This means that what we divine of providence from the obscurity represented by the table should not result in "metaphysic taking private illumination from intellectual institutions and thence regulating merely her own moral institutions." Instead, "metaphysic should know God's providence in public moral institutions or civil customs, by which the nations have come into being and maintain themselves in the world" (5).

From the breast of metaphysic the elements reflect onto the statue of Homer, illustrating the way metaphysics, guided by the elementi, descends further into particular human things, enabling us to return to "the beginning according to a history of human ideas from the commencing of truly human thinking." This return, then, is a descent "into the crude minds of the first founders of the gentile nations, all robust sense and vast imagination" (6). The elementi, Vico tells us, allow us to deduce the method by which the science proceeds (41). The degnità, the thoughts worth thinking, illuminate Vico's method or the path of his anabasis.

As degnità, the elementi are gnomic enthymemes, meant to engage the ingenium of the reader and enable him to recall the middle terms of human making and unite them in a narrative of providence. As thoughts proper and worthy for a human being to consider, the elementi enthymemically suggest an understanding of things human and divine in speech, which addresses the whole. In enabling us to address the whole, the degnità are the axioms of eloquent speech.

Eloquence is a criterion explicitly opposed to the criteria of clarity and distinctness which distinguish the Cartesian path of thinking. That path would unthinkingly apply the same general methodology of abstract thought to any and all areas of concern. Vico writes in contrast that "nature and life are full of incertitude; the foremost, indeed the only aim of our arts is to assure us that we have acted rightly. . . . Those who know all the *loci* . . . are able (by an operation not unlike reading the printed characters on a page) to group extemporaneously the elements of persuasion inherent in any question or case" (*SM* 15/799).

The elements, which are the equivalents of the printed characters on the page, are Vico's axioms. Vico in his axioms makes plain for us the "alphabet" of human culture, which will enable us to read off the patterns of providence and compose an eloquent narrative that addresses the whole.

The Cartesian thinker seeks to prove abstract truths through abstract axioms, in this way elaborating a chain of deductions in support of the point at issue. But according to Vico, this method is applicable only in its own rather discrete province. Applied outside those boundaries, in areas not amenable to such treatment, a curious situation can result: "There is no thesis here that is not subject to debate . . . so such verbal formulas as 'by definition IV,' 'by postulate II,' 'by axiom III,' and conclusions with the pompous abbreviation 'QED' . . . [have] none of the force of truth upon the mind . . . . Hence when someone proudly claims on behalf of a method that has no logically compulsive force, 'This is an axiom'; 'This is demonstrated'; he seems to me to be like a painter who writes beneath shapeless images that could never be made out on their own, 'This is a man'; 'This is a lion'; 'This is something else" (R 181/165). In this inverted world, an axiom becomes an index of madness and perversion—and the claim to clarity and certainty, an indisputable proof of the madness of the deductive madman.

Vico's axioms are instead degnità, whose proper and worthy province is that of the *Deutlichkeit* of which Hamann spoke, which consists in a realm of balanced lights and shadows in the indefinite provinces of the human mind. Vico means for his axioms to recall the primal images of the living human world, and they are in this way immediately identifiable to the thinker qua living human being. So argument in the *Scienza nuova* is not "the disposition of a proof" but is "that third term that one finds in order to unify the two arguments of a proposed problem . . . [and] more than this . . . is the art by which truth is apprehended, because it is the art of seeing under all the topical heads whatever there is in the matter at issue, which will enable us to distinguish well and have an adequate concept of it" (R 178/162). These "topical heads" become in the new science Vico's axioms, which like the alphabet in a book, allow us to discern patterns which contribute to the comprehension of the whole.

When we meditate Vico's axioms, we return to the originary makings which are constitutive of what it means to be human; they are, as

Verene puts it, "the very being of the thinker and the human world."[79] These axioms are the "ties that bind" human things into a history, a pattern of providence and human making that one can address eloquently—that is, comprehensively—as a whole. "It is these ties that are the beautiful ornaments of eloquence which make subtleties delightful" (A 123/12).

As we contemplate death's pageants in the eloquent theater of memory, the axioms, like the loci of the ancient memory systems, remind us of things we should know in narrating an eloquent whole. We view the axioms *in spettacolo*, in a theater, just as did the scholars who entered Camillo's theater.[80] Verene notes that "each axiom must be mastered, as must each image on the gates and grades of Camillo's theater. . . . We must meditate on these axioms until they become an inner writing whereby we can read off the life of any nation in terms of its divine pattern. . . . We glimpse the commonplace, the *topos*, from which the event is evoking itself."[81]

In this way the axioms become pisteis, means of persuasion, by which we come to understand the realities of our situation. The audience to be brought to a *krisis* is the reader of whom Vico speaks in the section on method (section IV of Book I): "Thus the proper and continual proof here adduced will consist in comparing and reflecting whether our human mind, in the series of possibilities it is permitted to understand, and so far as it is permitted to do so, can conceive more or fewer or different causes than those from which issue the effects of this civil world. In doing this the reader will experience in his mortal body a divine pleasure" (345).

He adds, directly addressing the reader in a passage I have invoked throughout this study, that just as geometry creates a world out of its elementi, so does "our Science, but with a reality greater by just so much as the things having to do with human affairs are more real than points, lines, surfaces, and figures are. And this very fact is an argument, O reader, that these proofs are of a kind divine and should give thee a divine pleasure" (349).

Now the full force of this passage should be clear. Reader, author, and the full "speech situation," or *status*, are being addressed in the *Scienza nuova* in a complete rhetorical sense. Vico is giving us in his axiomatic method a new kind of rhetorical demonstration that employs the degnità as enthymeme for one of "the artistic ways of proceeding concerning the means of persuasion" (*Rh* 1355a4). The body of persuasion is the text as a whole through which the degnità circulate, impelled by the ingenium of the readers, who meditate these cose to themselves and reache toward the invention of an eloquent whole.

Axioms I–XXII (and CVI) are the general topics, which as *koinoi* apply to any species of human knowledge, while axioms XXXIII–CXIV are the *eidē*, the particular topics, that offer the material the koinoi structure as intelligibles. The general axioms as topics are the ways into which the mind naturally falls when considering the particulars or certains.

So Vico states in axiom I that "because of the indefinite nature of the human mind" (120), or in axiom II that "it is another property of the human mind" (122), and so forth. A general axiom applied to a particular makes the two, as Grimaldi states of Aristotelian topics, "sources, or focal points, to be examined in order that one may deduce all . . . the varied particular aspects of any individual subject."[82] The certains of philology are brought into focus through the general axioms as they interact with the particular.

The general axioms as koinoi connect the diverse certains of particular customs, laws, or language in a quick and comprehensive way, allowing us to apply philosophy to philology in the manner of Aristotle's *Rhetoric*. Recall Aristotle's statement that "as in philosophy, too, it is characteristic of a well-aimed mind to see the likeness even in widely separated things" (*Rh* 1412a12–13). Res and verba interpenetrate in an eloquent narration which we meditate to ourselves from the elementi of the *Scienza nuova*.

Recall also that Aristotle explained: "I mean by 'element' and 'topic' the same thing" (*Rh* 1403a17) and that Theophrastus defined the topos as "some sort of governing root or element."[83] These definitions can now be connected with Vico's statement in the *Institutes* that "loci sunt veluti elementa arguendi [topics are as it were the elements of argument]" (*IO* 50). The axioms as topics are the elements of archaic logic, arguing from the beginnings of humanity in the master images that formed the human world.

The axioms, moreover, are gnomic. Aeschines' statement that "we learn the maxims of the poets carefully when we are children . . . that we may use them when we are men" can be taken in a conceit to illustrate this.[84] The maxims of the poets represent the sensory topics hewn out of the flux the first humans faced in the childhood of the race. They were absorbed over the ages through custom, making up the sensus communis. Now, through memoria, we recall them in the age of men, and we see their "reasons" under the particular guise they take in civil life.

A "maxim" qua sensory topic, as an element of social life, embodies the complex social and cultural web that the proairesis, or moral choice, of the first humans set in motion. Recall that *proairesis* primarily means "choosing one thing before another" and thus came to signify "preference" or "deliberate choice."[85] The cose that made us human were precisely such things. Aristotle also stated in the *Rhetoric* that there were maxims "with the 'supplementary reason'" and those "without the 'supplementary reason'" (*Rh* 1394b8) and that maxims without the supplementary reason could be converted into enthymemes through the addition of the logos (*Rh* 1393a21–23).

The "maxims" of the first age, which reflected the deliberate choice of the first humans in simple ignorance of the logos, become the degnità of the *Scienza nuova* when that logos is added in an awareness of precisely what a human being is, that is to say, in the light of self-knowledge. This logos is the science of recollective fantasia, the understanding of the primal mind that Vico called the master key of his new science. It understands that what makes us human is not tied up with logos qua reason and concept but qua imagination and image. For as Vico writes, "'logic' comes from *logos*, whose first and proper meaning was *fabula*, fable" (401). It is then *muthos* (myth) that most fully signifies "*vera narratio*, or true speech" (401). What Vico offers in his new science are the axioms of human making, as he limns the patterns and contours of the human imagination.

9 Conclusion: Heroic Wisdom

Human reality reflects a tension between the two poles of reason and feeling: between abstract reason and the realm of feeling rooted in our nature as bodily and social beings. This essential tension reflects the two-sided nature of human discourse. A verbal image of it can be found in the degnità, which circulate through Vico's *Scienza nuova*. How can the axiom as image in the microcosm be more clearly related to the macrocosm of the world Vico is trying to divine? And what are the archai of the balancing act we find in the axiom as gnomic enthymeme? What is the truth of Vico's act of human making? How does the witty image relate to the making that is structured in terms of the human whole—that making which, in addressing the whole, is eloquent, and thus *sapienza che parla*, or wisdom speaking? For when we find sapienza che parla, we find *parlare in concetti*, the witty and ironic speech of the maxim.

Here we make our final descent: we follow Vico through the diploid degnità of the maker's imagination to the origin of human knowing in the noetic poiēsis of the first human beings. In so doing, what do we learn? What is the wisdom we ultimately find as the basis of Vico's theater of memory and wisdom?

Poetic Wisdom

For Vico, as I discussed in Chapter 3, all thinking, all discourse, is ultimately traceable back to the experience of the first humans in forming "the commencing of truly human thinking" (6). And in tracing how that thinking developed, axiom LXIV must be adhered to: "The order of ideas must proceed according to the order of things" (238).[1]

So it is in the experience of "these first men, stupid, insensate, and horrible beasts" (374), that we must look for an account of human wisdom and knowledge: "The first sages were the theological poets, and

. . . the nature of [all] things that are ever born or made [la natura delle cose che sono mai nate o fatte] betrays the crudeness of its origins. It is thus and not otherwise that we must conceive the origins of poetic wisdom" (361). If we are to understand the tension inherent in the diploid maxim, we must look to the birth of poetic wisdom for its origin.

Vico tells us that "wisdom in general" is "the faculty that commands all the disciplines by which we acquire all the sciences and the arts which achieve humanity" (364). *Sapienza poetica* enabled the insensate *bestioni* to make the things that in turn made these beasts human. It was poetic wisdom that ruled when they made themselves human.

Such a wisdom, which perfects humanity, does so in an essential relation to our double nature, which consists of intellect and will. Vico states that "man, in his proper being as man, consists of mind and spirit, or, if we prefer, of intellect and will. It is the function of wisdom to fulfill both these parts in man" (364). It does so through an interplay between knowledge of divine and human things; an interplay of scienza and coscienza that results in distinctively human knowledge.

Arbor Scientiae

After explaining "Wisdom in General" in chapter I of Book II of the *Scienza nuova*, Vico proceeds in chapter II to the "Exposition and Division of Poetic Wisdom." And to explain the divisions, he makes use of the image of the tree of knowledge. He says: "We must trace the beginnings of poetic wisdom to a crude metaphysics. From this point, as from a trunk, there branch out from one limb logic, morals, economics, and politics, all poetic; and from another, physics, the mother of cosmography and astronomy, the latter of which gives their certainty to its two daughters, chronology and geography—all likewise, poetic" (367).

As Giorgio Tagliacozzo notes, the image of a tree of knowledge has a long tradition.[2] Frances Yates traces the first recorded use of the image (with reference to the art of memory) to Raymond Lull, the medieval master of mnemonics, who had "a fondness for diagrams in the form of trees."[3] In his *Arbor scientiae* Lull includes a diagram of a tree that symbolizes "the whole encyclopedia of knowledge."[4] Giordono Bruno then took up the image in *De umbris idearum*, his work on memory, placing under his fourth and fifth "seal" a tree and a forest that, "representing all knowledge, are rooted in the basic principles common to all."[5]

But regardless of whether Vico took his image from the hermetic tradition, it is clear that he was familiar with it from Bacon, who uses it in Book III of *De dignatate et augmentis scientiarum*.[6] Bacon notes there that "the divisions of knowledge are not like several lines that meet in one angle, but are rather like branches of a tree that meet in one stem (which stem grows for some distance entire and continuous, before it divides itself into arms and boughs)."[7] He adds that before considering the branches, we must look to the trunk; we must "erect and constitute one universal science to be the mother of the rest, and to be regarded in the progress of knowledge as portions of the main and common way, before we come where the ways part and divide themselves."[8] Bacon calls this trunk *Philosophia Prima*, primitive or summary philosophy, or *Sapience*, which was formerly defined as the knowledge of things divine and human."[9]

Descartes had a tree, too, although it was not involved, like those of Bacon and Vico, with the notion of a *sapientia* of things human and divine. As Verene notes, the difference between Descartes's and Vico's tree is instructive.[10]

The Cartesian tree is found in the letter Descartes wrote to the translator of the French version of *The Principles of Philosophy*, which originally appeared in Latin. There, Descartes claims that "philosophy as a whole is like a tree whose roots are metaphysics, whose trunk is physics, and whose branches, which issue from this trunk, are all the other sciences. These reduce themselves to three principal ones, viz., medicine, mechanics, and morals—I mean the highest and most perfect moral science which, presupposing a complete knowledge of the other sciences, is the last degree of wisdom."[11]

Descartes's tree is monologic. It moves from metaphysics through physics to morals in a straight line, following the upward thrust of knowledge.[12] But in Vico's tree physics is the science of only one branch, with the other containing the arts of humanity. Vico's tree is diploid. As Verene notes, it "embodies the division between nature and culture."[13] It takes account of the twofold direction of human nature and knowing, directed as it is both to the *coscienza* of the divine and the *scienza* of the human.

The trunk of Vico's tree is that *rozza metafisica* of the body I explained in Chapter 1. It is rooted in the basic experience of thunder as Jove, the master imaginative universal that forms the initial human "place" and starts the formation of both humanity and the human world. Fantasia is the heart of the trunk of poetic wisdom in the first age, while recollective fantasia takes its place in the third age.[14]

The initial creative activity in the first age took two basic directions in its opening moments. Vico notes that "at length the sky broke forth in thunder, and Jove thus gave a beginning to the world of men by arousing in them the conatus which is proper to the liberty of the mind, just as from motion, which is proper to bodies as necessary agents, he began the world of nature" (689).

One motion results in culture, and the other in nature, and each developed from the action of the imaginative universal. Verene explains that "the poetic sciences are a mode of human experience, but they are that part of the mind directed to a knowledge of the natural object which cannot itself be made in the scientific act of making it intelligible."[15] The arts are directed toward the things we do make, the human *cose*, which we can know as true.

Vico states that "the first languages in the first mute times of the nations must have begun with signs, whether gestures or physical objects, which had a natural relation to the ideas expressed" (401). Ernst Cassirer notes that in the theory of language as expressive movement, "two forms of gesture are usually distinguished, the *indicative* and the *imitative;* these classes can be clearly delimited both as to content and psychological genesis."[16]

The indicative gesture has its source in the physical motion of arms and hands in grasping and mastering objects. Cassirer cited W. Wundt, who in *Die Sprache: Volkerpsychologie*, notes that from the original use of the "grasping organs" to control and manipulate objects comes a gradual transformation of the grasping movement, which is eventually "attenuated to an indicative gesture."[17]

Wundt then cites, in a move Vico would appreciate, the experience of children to illustrate his thesis. It seems that the development of children recapitulates original genesis: "The child still clutches for objects that he cannot reach because they are too far away. In such cases, the clutching movement changes to a pointing movement. Only after repeated efforts to grasp the objects does the pointing movement as such establish itself."[18]

This indicative gesture, or "clutching at a distance," is one of the first ways the human being develops into a perceiving "I" with a perceived content separated out into an "objective" content. In this way conceptual knowledge has its rude birth in the immediacy of sensory grasping and pointing; rude empiricists, we want to grasp what we know with our hands.[19]

Cassirer notes that as "objective" conceptual knowledge develops, the sensory content becomes increasingly abstract—although it remains the epistemological root. He states:

> Both genetically and actually, there seems to be a
> continuous transition from physical to conceptual
> "grasping." Sensory-physical grasping becomes
> sensory interpretation, which in turn conceals within
> it the first impulse toward the higher functions of
> signification manifested in language and thought.
> We might suggest the scope of this development by
> saying that it leads from the sensory extreme of mere
> "indication" (*Weisen*) to the logical extreme of "dem-
> onstration" (*Beweisen*). From the mere indication by
> which an absolutely single thing (a *todeti* in the
> Aristotelian sense) is designated, the road leads to a
> progressively general specification: what in the begin-
> ning was a mere deictic function becomes the
> function of "apodeixis."[20]

The line is thus continuous from the first mute pointing at the sky to the abstract Cartesian world of extension and motion.

The second fundamental gesture is imitative. In this gesture the "outside" is not set off and pointed at; experience is not externalized but internalized in a reproductive, imitative manner. But such an imitation is not a mere copying (as if there were external objects that could be internally reproduced); human experience at any level is creative, rooted in fantasia. Cassirer points to Aristotle's notion that the inarticulate sound that expresses the animal's sensation becomes articulate, linguistic sound only through its use as a symbol.[21] Mimesis thus belongs to poiēsis and is no mere repetition: "The apparent 'reproduction' (*Nachbilden*) actually presupposes an inner 'production' (*Vorbilden*)."[22]

The mimetic function is rooted in the maker's imagination, expressing a second fundamental direction of human world-making. Cassirer writes that "this reproduction never consists in retracing, line for line, a specific content of reality; but in selecting a pregnant motif in that content and so producing a characteristic 'outline' of its form. . . . To reproduce an object in this sense means not merely to compose it from its particular sensuous characteristics, but to apprehend it in its structural relations which can only be truly understood if the consciousness constructively produces them."[23]

The moments of the imitative and the indicative are essentially related. Cassirer notes that "even though sensuous and spiritual elements seem to have been inextricably intertwined in the origins of language, this *correlation*, precisely because it is a correlation, does not argue a relation of *one-sided* dependency between the two. For intellectual expression could not have developed through and out of sensuous expression if it had not originally been contained in it; if, as Herder said, sensuous designation did not already embrace a basic act of 'reflection.'"[24]

The origin of this essential opposition, according to Vico, is discovered in the founding experience of Jove. The sky thundered, and the bestioni both trembled and pointed. In their fear they took up the world into themselves, and in their wonder they set themselves off from it. It was their ingenium, their wit, that made a narrative whole of this opposition under the sovereign direction of fantasia. Through the maker's imagination they created enthymemic fables that united the world in wit.

Both the deictic and the mimetic functions are contained within the mute language that developed from the master imaginative universal of Jove. Verene notes that "Jove can be apprehended as nature, pointed at and affixed in the sky. He can also be read as a sign, imitated in a ritual of fearful shaking. In the mimetic gesture or ritual act Jove can be transferred as a meaning into a different medium. He is grasped as metaphor."[25] He is the middle term in the original and originary enthymeme, which can be recollected through the elementi of the *Scienza nuova*.

The mimetic apprehension of Jove gives us the branch of the tree that represents the poetic arts, while the indicative apprehension of Jove gives us the branch of the poetic sciences. The mimetic apprehension is based on the verum-factum principle, and it results in a scienza of the cose made by human beings; a knowledge of things human (one half of wisdom).[26]

The branch of the sciences, which starts with physics, represents coscienza of the divine cose. Because we cannot make these things, we then have no knowledge (scienza) of them, but only consciousness (coscienza). We can only be conscious of nature, pointing to it and understanding it in terms of an extension of our own body, but we can never make it and make it true. This is the knowledge of things divine—the other half of wisdom's province, which rules both.[27] This is what is divined by the new seers of Vico's science, as they follow the method the elementi mark out in the descent from the eye of providence.

Externalizing and internalizing poiēsis should not, then, be subsumed under each other, because they reciprocally determine the human world. One branch of the tree is concerned with images, the other with concepts. Mimetic truth is an "inside" truth, because we make its things; while indicative truth is only a certainty, an "outside" truth rooted in the witnessing consciousness. Both are combined in Vico's axiomatics.

Verene observes that "the poetic sciences and arts are two polar activities of mind that make up the whole of mind in its original state. But there is no common element of unity in which they share. Mind is by nature a duality, but it is a whole in that each of its branches reciprocally determines the nature of the other. Mind is this activity. Jove is not an internal principle of unity of mind because his appearance always has two aspects. Jove is manifest in two types of signs. He is not a sign any more than pointing is imitating."[28] The activity of mind is enthymemic: it is a well-regulated excess that balances between the mimetic and indicative functions.

Vico's axiomatics is enthymemic as well, operating under the general principle of the well-regulated excess symbolized by Demosthenes. It is an axiomatics of organic discourse that eloquently addresses pragma, ēthos, and pathos in the great city of the human race.

But Vico's axiomatics is also temporally situated: it is an axiomatics that takes account of the flux that will not stand still. Under Vico's rubric, there are three ages, which are determined by the essential opposition between these two ways of knowing: the ages of gods, heroes, and men. Three languages also result from the central opposition of knowing, corresponding to these three ages. But the three languages, as a function of the bipolar opposition, are present, at least in germ, in the beginning as well as the end. Vico writes that "to enter now upon the extremely difficult way in which these three kinds of languages and letters were formed, we must establish this principle: that as gods, heroes, and men began at the same time (for there were, after all, men who imagined the gods and believed their own heroic nature to be a mixture of the divine and human natures), so these three languages began at the same time" (446).

But the account of how these three ages and languages come about is developmental, arising out of a dialectic between the indicative and the mimetic. Vico notes that the languages "began, however, with these three very great differences: that the language of gods was almost entirely mute, only very slightly articulate; the language of heroes, an equal mixture of articulate and mute . . . and the language of men, almost entirely articulate and only very slightly mute" (446).

The age of the gods is almost entirely dominated by the imaginative universal, to the virtual exclusion of abstract thought. One pole of thought is ascendant, the other in its shadow. In the last age there is a reversal of this, and the abstract universal is ascendant. There is a movement from the mute image to the abstract shout, with a whole continuum of stages in between. And at the midpoint, the age of heroes, there was an unself-conscious balance between the two, symbolized for Vico by Demosthenes, who was "armed with his invincible enthymeme" (*AR* 87/939).

But this is a balance that will not remain in stasis but will inevitably decline into the ever-growing clamor of the concept.

What is the role of third-age wisdom in all of this? For wisdom is the ruling discipline, which teaches us how to operate in terms of how things are. If sapienza allows a self-knowledge of this bipolar structure through Vichian axiomatics in the time of the third age, what does it allow us to know and do?

A Geometry of Melancholy

Wisdom sits outside the spectacle of death's pageants, viewing the dialectic between the two poles of human existence. She views an inevitable *corso* that begins brightly and colorfully and full of gods and slowly runs down and bleaches itself bare-bones white: a inevitable march from the ferment of enthusiasm to the exactness of the contentless concept.[29] Furnished with the ticket of Vichian axiomatics, Wisdom enters the Theater of Memory.

Wisdom cannot fully join herself either to the insensate imagination of the first humans or to the transparent consciousness of the last ones. The two are equally lacking in self-knowledge; neither acknowledges the trunk of sapienza poetica, which is rooted in fantasia, common to each. The heroic mind lacks actualized self-knowledge as well; yet, as a balance between the two poles of human being-in-the-world, it is an emblem for the stance wisdom seeks to attain.

Wisdom watches while the frenzied enthusiasm of the ancients declines into the dissolute wit of the moderns, and watches, too, the quarrel between those who are nostalgic for the frenzy and those decadent enough to be satisfied "with only the bare feeling of the divine in general."[30] To become a partisan of nostalgia is self-defeating, for we live in the third age. As Vico noted, the attempted return to ancient sources ironically ended in scholasticism. And the equally obtuse reaction against the ancients only compounds the modern dilemma (*AR* 85–86/938).

In the attempt to balance between the two, Wisdom issues forth in a geometry of melancholy. Wisdom cannot make the world, only recall its making. Denied the comedy of reform, she demonstrates to herself the pattern of the ideal eternal history and does not smile. Wisdom watches the pattern but does not imitate it. She takes instead the path of descent that is also an ascent. She follows the path of Vico's anabasis.

Vico states in axiom LII that human beings "at first feel without perceiving, then they perceive with a troubled and agitated spirit, finally they reflect with a clear mind" (218). He adds as a corollary that "this axiom is the principle of poetic sentences, which are formed by feelings of passion and emotion, whereas philosophic sentences are formed by reflection and reasoning. The more the latter rise toward universals, the closer they approach the truth; the more the former descend to particulars, the more certain they become" (219).

Vico's geometry of melancholy teaches us that we must seek for a self-aware balance between the twin barbarisms of sense and reflection, which arise when we adhere exclusively to one or the other poles of our essential nature. We must not embrace too readily either the rapturous haziness of the sensuous depths or the monochromatic formalism that forever mutters the same thing to itself.[31] The attempt to balance between them is pictured in the axiomatic method of the *Scienza nuova*, which is best understood through the lightning strike of the invincible enthymeme.

Notes

Preface

1. Alasdair MacIntyre, "Imaginative Universals and Historical Falsification: A Rejoinder to Professor Verene," *New Vico Studies* 6 (1988): 22, 26.

2. Isaiah Berlin, *Vico and Herder* (New York: Viking, 1976), 67.

3. René Descartes, *Philosophical Works of Descartes*, Vol. 1, trans. E. S. Haldane and G. R. T. Ross (New York: Dover, 1955), 85.

4. Giambattista Vico, *The New Science of Giambattista Vico*, trans. M. H. Fisch and T. G. Bergin (Ithaca, N.Y.: Cornell University Press, 1984); *La scienza nuova seconda*, ed. F. Nicolini, in *Opere di G.B. Vico*, Vol. 4 (Bari: Laterza, 1942). Further references to Vico's *New Science* are to these editions and are cited parenthetically in the text by Nicolini's paragraph enumeration, which is common to both editions. I have occasionally modified the translation to bring out a particular emphasis in the Italian.

5. Heraclitus, in R. Wright, *The Presocratics: The Main Fragments in Greek* (Bristol: Bristol Classical Press, 1985). Further references are to this edition and will be cited parenthetically in the text by the standard fragment numbering. Unless otherwise noted, all translations of this and other Greek texts are my own.

6. The title *Scienza nuova*, or *New Science*, denotes the *Scienza nuova seconda*, the title Vico used for the second edition (1730); it has been used since the edition by Fausto Nicolini to refer to this and to the third edition of 1744. The first edition, of 1725, will be referred to as the *Scienza nuova prima*, or the first *New Science*. When I use the term "new science," I am referring to Vico's thought itself, as it came to fruition in the *New Science*, and not to the text of the 1730/1744 edition.

7. Owen Barfield, *Poetic Diction* (Scranton, Pa.: Harper and Row, 1973), 133.

8. See ibid., 168–177; 206. Barfield's work is not on Vico, but independently rediscovers and restates many Vichian themes on poetic experience and the imagination. For Barfield's comments on his discovery of Vico after writing his book, see 219.

9. The phrase is Nancy Struever's, in *Theory as Practice: Ethical Inquiry in the Renaissance* (Chicago: University of Chicago Press, 1992), xii.

Chapter 1: Vico's Anabasis

1. Henry George Liddell and Robert Scott, *A Greek-English Lexicon*. Rev. and augmented Henry Stuart Jones (Oxford: Clarendon, 1968), entry under *katabainō*.

2. Ibid., entry under *anabainō*.

3. Max H. Fisch, introduction to Giambattista Vico, *The New Science of Giambattista Vico*, trans. M. H. Fisch and T. G. Bergin (Ithaca, N.Y.: Cornell University Press, 1984), xx.

4. Here I translate *cose* as "things" rather than "institutions," as Bergin and Fisch do, in order to bring out the general applicability of the axioms to any particular aspect of human nature or culture, any *certo*, which has a birth and a growth as a product of the poiēsis of *fantasia* (*institutions* suggests perhaps a more *rational* stage of human making). As Fisch notes, Vico consciously chose *not* to use the common Italian word for *institutions* because he wanted to emphasize the arational origin of human culture. Fisch argues that *institution* is not a loaded word in our time and thus can be safely used. As a survivor of several undergraduate sociology classes, I find I have reason to disagree, and follow Vico's usage instead. On this see Fisch's introduction, xliii–xlv.

5. See Donald Phillip Verene, "The New Art of Narration: Vico and the Muses," *New Vico Studies* 1 (1983): 21–38.

6. Giambattista Vico, *The Autobiography of Giambattista Vico*, trans. M. H. Fisch and T. G. Bergin (Ithaca, N.Y.: Cornell University Press, 1990), 119/*Vico: Opere Filosofiche*, ed. Paolo Cristofolini (Firenze: Sansoni, 1971), 9. Further references are to these editions and are cited parenthetically in the text after the abbreviation *A*; the first page number refers to the English text, the second to the Italian. Further citations from Vico's works will appear parenthetically in the text with the same citation style (see list of abbreviations) and refer to the following editions: *The Academies and the Relation between Philosophy and Eloquence*, trans. Donald Phillip Verene, in *On the Study Methods of Our Time*, trans. Elio Gianturco (Ithaca, N.Y.: Cornell University Press, 1990)/*Vico: Opere*, ed. Fausto Nicolini (Milan: Riccardo Ricciardi, 1953); *On the Most Ancient Wisdom of the Italians*, trans. Lucia Palmer (Ithaca, N.Y.: Cornell University Press, 1988)/*Opere Filosofiche; Institutiones oratoriae*, ed. Giulio Crifò (Naples: Institute Suor Orsola Beninca, 1989); *Disputation with the Giornale de' letterati d'Italia*, trans. Lucia Palmer, in *On the Most Ancient Wisdom of the Italians/Opere Filosofiche; On the Study Methods of Our Time*, trans. Elio Gianturco (Ithaca, N.Y.: Cornell University Press, 1990)/*Opere Filosofiche*.

7. For such a history one need only consult the masterful Fausto Nicolini, who in his *Commento storico alla seconda Scienza Nuova*, Vols. 1 and 2 (Rome: Edizioni di Storia e Letteratura, 1978), has to a great extent done just that.

8. Donald Phillip Verene, *Vico's Science of the Imagination* (Ithaca, N.Y.: Cornell University Press, 1981), 125.

9. Michael Mooney, *Vico in the Tradition of Rhetoric* (Princeton: Princeton University Press, 1985), 12.

10. Ibid., 20.

11. Ibid., 23.

12. Ibid., 262–263.

13. Ibid., 263. I quote Berlin and MacIntyre in the Preface.

14. Karl-Otto Apel, *Die Idee der Sprache in der Tradition des Humanism von Dante bis Vico*, 2d ed. (Bonn: Bouvier Verlag Herbert Grundmann, 1975), 320–321.

15. Ernesto Grassi, *Rhetoric as Philosophy: The Humanistic Tradition* (University Park: Pennsylvania State University Press, 1980), 5.

16. Nancy S. Struever, "Rhetoric and Philosophy in Vichian Inquiry," *New Vico Studies* 3 (1985): 131–145.

17. Struever's article is an excellent critique of those who oversimplify Vico's *complicated* relation to the Renaissance.

18. Verene, *Vico's Science*, 30.

19. This is also true, of course, of the Renaissance itself. Struever notes that thinkers such analyses oversimplify the Renaissance, focusing on "the pedestrian, the unproblematic, the doggedly optimistic notions." See "Rhetoric and Philosophy," 135–138. Eugenio Garin also notes that Vico cannot be seen simply as a man of the late Renaissance, but must be considered in relation to the eighteenth century as well. See his "Vico and the Heritage of Renaissance Thought," in *Vico: Past and Present*, ed. G. Tagliacozzo (Atlantic Highlands, N.J.: Humanities, 1981), 99–116. Thus I choose as my guides into Renaissance philosophy thinkers like Grassi and Cassirer, both of whom seem to have a sense for the strange and the unfamiliar.

20. Nicholas of Cusa, *On Learned Ignorance*, trans. Jasper Hopkins (Minneapolis: Arthur J. Banning Press, 1985), 31. For the significance of Cusa to Renaissance thought, see Ernst Cassirer, *The Individual and the Cosmos in Renaissance Philosophy*, trans. Mario Domandi (Oxford: Basil Blackwell, 1963), 1–2. For Cassirer's remarks on the notion of the microcosm, see especially 40–42, 64–66, and 84.

21. See *The Cambridge History of Renaissance Philosophy*, ed. Charles B. Schmidt (Cambridge: Cambridge University Press, 1990), 552.

22. Paracelsus, *Paracelsus: Selected Writings*, trans. Jolande Jacobi (Princeton: Princeton University Press, 1973), 25.

23. Ibid., 154.

24. See Cassirer, *Individual and Cosmos*, 40.

25. *Cambridge History*, 553.

26. Cassirer, *Individual and Cosmos*, 41. Of course, Platonists are not the same as Plato.

27. Ibid., 43.

28. Ibid., 41.

29. Ibid.

30. *Cambridge History*, 553. Also see 310.

31. Nicholas of Cusa, *Ignorance*, 92. Also see *Cambridge History*, 552–554.

32. *Cambridge History*, 63.

33. Francesco da Diacetto, quoted in ibid., 312.

34. Cassirer, *Individual and Cosmos*, 64.

35. See ibid., 64–66; *Cambridge History*, 572–573.

36. Cassirer, *Individual and Cosmos*, 67.

37. Ibid.

38. Leonardo da Vinci, quoted in Cassirer, *Individual and Cosmos*, 67.

39. Ibid., 65–68.

40. Cassirer, *Individual and Cosmos*, 1.

41. See *Cambridge History*, 727.

42. Jerry Seigal, *Rhetoric and Philosophy in Renaissance Humanism* (Princeton: Princeton University Press, 1968), xi.

43. Isocrates, *Panegyricus*, 149 (Loeb edition; Norlin translation).

44. Cicero, *De partitione oratoria*, 23.79 (Loeb edition; Hubble translation). Also see *Cambridge History*, 61.

45. Grassi, *Rhetoric as Philosophy*, 50.

46. Ibid., 93.

47. Ibid., 91.

48. Charlton T. Lewis and Charles Short, *A Latin Dictionary* (Oxford: Clarendon Press, 1980), entry under *ornatus*.

49. Ibid.

50. Grassi, *Rhetoric as Philosophy*, 91.

51. Cassirer, *Individual and Cosmos*, 156.

52. Galileo, quoted in E. A. Burtt, *The Metaphysical Foundations of Modern Science* (New York: Doubleday, 1954), 75.

53. Cassirer, *Individual and Cosmos*, 157–158.

54. Ibid., 159.

55. Ibid., 158–160.

56. Ibid., 159–161.

57. See ibid., 161.

58. There is one other essential element, the great Renaissance idea of *prudentia*, or wisdom. The natural place for an exposition of that, however, will be in Chapter 5, where I discuss the issue of "artificial memory" and topical method. For, as we shall see, in the Renaissance, as in classical times, memory, topics, and wisdom are closely related.

Chapter 2: Eloquent Memory and Barbaric Clarity

1. Ernesto Grassi, *Rhetoric as Philosophy: The Humanistic Tradition* (University Park: Pennsylvania State University Press, 1980), 100.

2. Ibid., 113.

3. Donald Phillip Verene, "Gadamer and Vico on *Sensus Communis* and the Tradition of Humane Knowledge," forthcoming in *The Library of Living Philosophers* volume on Gadamer published by Open Court.

4. See Donald Phillip Verene, "Imaginative Universals and Narrative Truth," *New Vico Studies* 6 (1988): 1–19. Here I am not referring to the three principles of humanity (religion, marriage, and burial), which as *cose* men of course do make, but to the patterns in history these cose allow us to mark out (prominent among which are the patterns of the "Ideal Eternal History").

5. Ibid., 10.

6. See Verene, "Gadamer and Vico," 23.

Chapter 3: The Way Down

1. My interpretation of Vico in this chapter is based upon Donald Phillip Verene's work in *Vico's Science of the Imagination* (Ithaca, N.Y.: Cornell University Press, 1981), which offers an account of Vico's thought that places the maker's imagination and the imaginative universal as the basis of Vico's new science. This is something surprisingly new in Vico interpretation. Isaiah Berlin, in *Vico and Herder: Two Studies in the History of Ideas* (New York: Viking, 1976), is perhaps closest in his emphasis on imagination; but Berlin does not seem to fully appreciate the newness or philosophical significance of *fantasia* for Vico. Ferdinand Fellman, in *Das Vico-Axiom: Der Mensch Macht die Geschichte* (Freiburg: Verlag Karl Alber, 1976), discusses the imaginative universal, but only in the context of Vico's concept

of historical knowledge. Leon Pompa, in *Vico: A Study of the New Science* (Cambridge: Cambridge University Press, 1975), seems intent on viewing Vico through the distorting lenses of modern scientism, and thus also seems to miss the philosophical significance and centrality of imagination and the imaginative universal in Vico. According to Verene, imagination is viewed as a method of philosophical thought in Vico, rather than as an object of it. It is Verene's attempt to view Vico as a philosopher of recollective imagination—and thus as a philosopher who stands outside the Western tradition of philosophical thought—that underlies my thinking in this chapter.

2. Verene, *Vico's Science*, 81.

3. Ibid., 205.

4. Ibid., 72.

5. Ibid., 74.

6. See ibid., 75–76.

7. Also see ibid., 76–77.

8. Ibid., 76.

9. Owen Barfield, *Poetic Diction* (Scranton, Pa.: Harper and Row, 1973), 82. Vico continually uses the mentality of children—and peasants and native peoples—as a clue to the mentality of the first humans, who were "the children of the human race" (498). On this see Verene, *Vico's Science*, 70. Verene notes that the following sections of the *New Science* are relevant: 206–17, 375–76, 437, 470, 498, 517, 658, 708, 841, 1095.

10. Barfield, *Poetic Diction*, 82. Barfield describes what Vico would call the *boria de'dotti* thus: "A good name for this kind of banality—the fruit, as it is, of *projecting post-logical thoughts back into a pre-logical age*—would perhaps be *logomorphism* . . . the paramount necessity that the great Mumbo Jumbo, the patent, double-million magnifying Inductive Method, should be allowed to continue contemplating its own ideal reflection" (190).

11. Ibid., 82.

12. Willard Van Orman Quine, *Word and Object* (Cambridge: MIT Press, 1965), 120. Barfield's work was first published in 1928.

13. Ibid., 92.

14. Ibid.

15. Ibid., 122. Quine at this point cites Cassirer's *Language and Myth*.

16. Barfield, *Poetic Diction*, 85.

17. Quine, *Word and Object*, 123.

18. Barfield, *Poetic Diction*, 91.

19. See Joan Marie Lechner, *Renaissance Concepts of the Commonplaces* (New York: Pageant, 1962), 1–22. Also see Verene, *Vico's Science*, 170–171;

Aristotle: On Rhetoric, trans. George A. Kennedy (New York: Oxford University Press, 1991), 45–47, 190–220; Walter Jost, "Teaching the Topics," *Rhetorical Society Quarterly* 21 (Winter 1991): 1–16; Michael C. Leff, "The Topics of Argumentative Invention in Latin Rhetorical Thinking from Cicero to Boethius," *Rhetorica* 1 (Spring 1983): 23–44; and, of course, Chapters 5 and 6, below.

20. See Verene, *Vico's Science*, 80.

21. Ibid., 173.

22. Barfield, *Poetic Diction*, 147.

23. Ibid., 91.

24. Ibid., 206–207.

25. Irony presupposes reflection "because it is fashioned of falsehood by dint of a reflection which wears the mask of truth. . . . Since the first men of the gentile world had the simplicity of children who are truthful by nature the first fables could not feign anything false" but were "true and severe narrations" (408).

26. See Verene, *Vico's Science*, 82–83.

27. Ernesto Grassi, *Rhetoric as Philosophy: The Humanist Tradition* (University Park: Pennsylvania State University Press, 1980), 96.

28. Ibid., 97.

29. See ibid., 20.

30. Ibid.

31. See Verene, *Vico's Science*, 79–80.

32. Ibid., 83.

33. Ibid., 84.

34. See ibid., 83–85.

35. Ibid., 134.

36. See ibid., 128–136.

37. See Barfield, *Poetic Diction*, 168–177.

38. Ibid., 171.

39. See ibid., 206.

40. Only philosophers as *late* and *decadent* as Plato and Aristotle would think that true philosophy begins in wonder; though it is true enough that the reflective variety does so arise.

41. Barfield, *Poetic Diction*, 177.

Chapter 4: The Way Up

1. Owen Barfield, *Poetic Diction* (Scranton, Pa.: Harper and Row, 1973), 189.

2. Ibid., 106.

3. See ibid., 107.

4. See ibid., 211.

5. Ibid., 209.

6. See Donald Phillip Verene, *Vico's Science of the Imagination* (Ithaca, N. Y.: Cornell University Press, 1981), 100.

7. Also see ibid., 101.

8. Ibid.

9. Barfield, *Poetic Diction*, 107.

10. See Verene, *Vico's Science*, 104.

11. Ibid.

12. See ibid.

13. Ibid.

14. See Barfield, *Poetic Diction*, 168–177.

15. Verene, *Vico's Science*, 104.

16. See ibid., 105.

17. *The Cambridge Italian Dictionary*, Vol. 1, ed. Barbara Reynolds (Cambridge: Cambridge University Press, 1981), entry under *contornare*.

18. Ibid.

19. Verene, *Vico's Science*, 106.

20. Ibid., 99–100.

21. See ibid., 102.

22. Stephen H. Daniel, "Vico on Mythic Figuration," *New Vico Studies* 3 (1985): 61–72.

23. Ibid., 68–69.

24. Verene, *Vico's Science*, 102.

25. Ibid.

26. See ibid., 107.

27. See ibid., 108.

28. Ibid., 107–108.

29. Ibid., 106.

30. See Max H. Fisch, introduction to Giambattista Vico, *The New Science of Giambattista Vico*, trans. M. H. Fisch and T. G. Bergin (Ithaca, N. Y., 1984), xix.

31. Ibid., xx.

32. Ibid.

33. See ibid.

34. Also see ibid., xxv.

35. See ibid., xxiii.

36. Verene, *Vico's Science*, 109.

37. Ibid.

38. See ibid.

39. See ibid., 109.

40. Ibid.

41. Ibid.

42. See ibid., 110.

43. Ibid.

44. See ibid.

45. Ernst Cassirer, *The Logic of the Humanities*, trans. C. S. Howe (New Haven: Yale University Press, 1971), 54.

46. Isaiah Berlin, *Vico and Herder: Two Studies in the History of Ideas* (New York: Viking, 1976), 67.

Chapter 5: The Roots of Rhetoric

1. Donald Phillip Verene, *The New Art of Autobiography: An Essay on the Life of Giambattista Vico Written by Himself* (Oxford: Clarendon, 1991), 127.

2. See Elio Gianturco, "Translator's Introduction," in *SM*, xxxiii–xxxvi. Also see Verene, *New Art*, 128–129.

3. Here, of course, "ancient and modern" is a master metaphor, standing for various approaches to knowing that were present, in germ at least, in antiquity, and became full blown in Vico's time. I am thinking not in terms of chronology but of origins. On this see Verene, *New Art*, 129.

4. The relevance of these passages is pointed out by Verene, ibid., 128.

5. Ibid., 129–130.

6. As Verene points out, the title by which *De nostri temporis studiorum ratione* has come to be known in its English translation, *On the Study Methods of Our Time*, is not quite accurate. For *studiorum* is plural, and *ratione* is singular, giving us "method of studies" rather than "study methods." Vico is not concerned with algorithmic procedures but with an organizing principle; concerned to trace a governing root rather than an assemblage of ends-oriented techniques. See Verene, "Preface," in *SM*, xii–xiii.

7. See Verene, *New Art*, 131–133, for a consideration of Vico's opposition to analysis that is artificially divorced from topical invention.

8. Here again we have a master metaphor: Greek philosophy represents in Western imagination the condition of wholeness present at the origin. Socrates becomes a locus of this belief, a sort of imaginative universal of the philosopher in

the Western tradition. Vico plays the notes of such tropes as these like a master musician of the imagination. On the role of Socrates as ideal portrait, see Verene, *New Art*, 78–81.

9. See Verene, ibid., 74.

10. Giambattista Vico, "Oratio I," in *Opere Filosofiche*, ed. Paolo Cristofolini (Firenze: Sansoni, 1971), 709.

11. See Verene, *New Art*, 74.

12. René Descartes, "Meditation III," in *Philosophical Works of Descartes*, Vol. 1, trans. E. S. Haldane and G. R. T. Ross (New York: Dover, 1955), 157.

13. Joan Marie Lechner, *Renaissance Concepts of the Commonplaces* (New York: Pageant, 1962), 237.

14. See general axioms XV and CVI.

15. See Lechner, *Renaissance Concepts*, 1–2.

16. See George A. Kennedy in *Aristotle: On Rhetoric*, trans. George A. Kennedy (New York: Oxford University Press, 1991), 45.

17. Ibid.

18. This is, of course, the essence of the dialectical method. On Aristotle's attempts to mediate common beliefs whenever possible, see Terence Irwin's glossary to Aristotle, *Nicomachean Ethics*, trans. Terence Irwin (Indianapolis: Hackett, 1985), 397–398.

19. William J. Grimaldi, *Studies in the Philosophy of Aristotle's* Rhetoric (Wiesbaden: Steiner, 1975), 122. Also see 119–123.

20. Ibid.

21. Lechner, *Renaissance Concepts*, 1–3.

22. Cicero, *Topica*, II.7–8 (Loeb edition; Hubbell translation).

23. See Lechner, *Renaissance Concepts*, 17.

24. Ibid.

25. Ibid., 3.

26. Ibid., 131.

27. Ibid., 136.

28. Ibid., 150–151.

29. Ibid., 151.

30. See Lechner, *Renaissance Concepts*, 13–14. Lechner defines sophistic dialectic solely in terms of argument and does not discuss its epistemological and ontological implications, which my phrase on the double or twofold character of reality points to. Lechner seems to accept the characterization of the early Sophists as merely cunning and self-serving (ironically, the traditional commonplace from which to consider the Sophists!).

31. Diogenes, quoted in Edward Schiappa, *Protagoras and Logos: A Study in Greek Philosophy and Rhetoric* (Columbia: University of South Carolina Press, 1991), 89 (=DL 9.51). As Schiappa notes, Diogenes introduces the fragment with the words *kai prōtos ephē* (and he said), which imply that the fragment is a quotation. Similar reports are also offered by Clement of Alexandria and Seneca, which indicates that even if Diogenes is paraphrasing, the actual words must have included the key notions of logoi, opposition, and things (i.e., the fragment seems to be authentically Protagorean). See pages 89–90. On the question of how to translate this fragment see pages 90–92 and 98–100. I am obviously advocating what Schiappa calls the "Heraclitean" interpretation (i.e., that the two logoi are real aspects of the object of inquiry, not a subjective creation of the speaker, conditioned solely by his private and ulterior motives).

32. Mario Untersteiner, quoted in ibid., 91.

33. Note that in my "rehabilitation" of the early Sophistic, I do not claim that there were no eristics or self-serving rhetoricians (no more than one would say there are no bad doctors or engineers); my initial point is simply that the eristics and profiteers were inexcellent rhetoricians. The tradition of rhetoric I am tracing here, from its Sophistic roots through Isocrates and Aristotle, Cicero and Quintillian, down to Vico, is concerned with the art of presenting human realities in a way commensurate with the human condition, i.e., in a true and human way. On this see Grimaldi, *Studies in Aristotle's* Rhetoric, 1–7, and my discussion of Aristotle's *Rhetoric*, below.

34. Grimaldi, *Studies in Aristotle's* Rhetoric, 7.

35. Ibid., 4.

36. Frances Yates, *The Art of Memory* (Chicago: Chicago University Press, 1966), 8–9, points to this distinction in Cicero, though she does not view the possible connection with Protagoras or the early growth of rhetoric as I am developing it.

37. Cicero, *De inventione*, I.viii.9 (Loeb edition; here I follow the translation offered by Yates, *Art of Memory*, 9, which follows the Latin more literally).

38. Yates, ibid.

39. See Lechner, *Renaissance Concepts*, 14.

40. Ibid.

41. See ibid., 4.

42. See ibid.

43. Cicero, *De inventione*, II.15.49–50 (Loeb edition; Hubbel translation).

44. Quintillian, *Institutiones oratoriae*, II.4.31 (Loeb edition; Butler translation). Also see Lechner, *Renaissance Concepts*, 4, 26.

45. Lechner, *Renaissance Concepts*, 16.

46. Isocrates, *Antidosis*, in *Isocrates* (Loeb edition: Norlin translation), 285.

47. George Norlin, "Translator's Introduction," in *Isocrates*, xxii. Also see Isocrates, *Against the Sophists*, in *Isocrates*, 17ff.

48. Lechner, *Renaissance Concepts*, 5.

49. Isocrates, *Antidosis*, 271. Also see 284; Isocrates, *Panath.*, in *Isocrates*, 28–30; Isocrates, *Against the Sophists*, 16; Isocrates, *Helen*, in *Isocrates*, 5.

50. Lechner, *Renaissance Concepts*, 6.

51. Kennedy, in *Aristotle: On Rhetoric*, vii.

52. Ibid.

53. Grimaldi, *Studies in Aristotle's* Rhetoric, 2–3.

54. See Lechner, *Renaissance Concepts*, 29.

55. Ibid., 30.

56. Ibid., 33.

57. See ibid., 41.

58. Ibid.

59. See ibid.

60. Cicero, *Orator*, XXXI.113–114 (Loeb edition; Hubbel translation).

61. Ibid., XXXI.114–15.

62. See ibid.

63. See Lechner, *Renaissance Concepts*, 101.

64. Ibid.

65. Phillipp Melanchthon, *Elementorum rhetorices libri duo* (1572), quoted in Lechner, *Renaissance Concepts*, 75. The rear guard is at its most vigorous in Melanchthon, and he does not really perceive in his nostalgia the storm about to break about its head with Galileo, Descartes, and Newton.

66. Valerius, *Philosophia vetus et nova ad usum scholae* (Paris, 1678), quoted in Lechner, *Renaissance Concepts*, 83.

67. Ibid., 85.

68. See Lechner, ibid., 7–8.

69. Ibid., 209–210.

70. Ibid., 7.

71. Christopher Maurer, "Translator's Introduction," in Baltasar Gracián, *The Art of Worldly Wisdom*, trans. Christopher Maurer (New York: Doubleday, 1992), xv. I shall return to Maurer's interesting description later, in Chapter 8, when I discuss the style of the *Scienza nuova* in more detail.

72. Aristotle, *Topics*, 105b (Loeb edition; my translation).

73. See Lechner, *Renaissance Concepts*, 155–161. Brinsley's *Ludus literarius* (1627) is cited as an example; Lechner notes that Brinsley is not at all singular in his dependence on the loci communes even in the simplest rhetorical exercise: "There is scarcely a Renaissance schoolmaster or rhetorician whose name could not be added to Brinsley's as advocator of intensive instruction in the assembling and use of the commonplaces" (161).

74. Ibid., 170. That it was known in Vico's time is evident from his statement in the *Autobiography* that in reading a book for the third time he read "in great detail to collect the fine turns of thought and expression, which he marked in the books themselves instead of copying them into commonplace or phrase books" (*A* 120/10).

75. See Lechner, *Renaissance Concepts*, 169.

76. Francis Bacon, quoted in Ibid., 172. Lechner notes of Bacon that "the early English essays show the influence of the commonplace book, being themselves little more than a collection of scattered meditations—quotations, sentences, anecdotes. . . . [In] the essays published by Bacon in 1597 . . . the aphorisms which he collected under headings represent the selections from one of his commonplace books" (217). Of course the *Novum organon* itself is a sequence of numbered aphorisms of varying length.

77. See Lechner, ibid., 173.

78. See Yates, *Art of Memory*, 1–2.

79. Cicero, *De oratoria*, II.lxxxvi.351–354 (Loeb edition; translation modified to follow the more literal translation offered by Yates, *Art of Memory*, 2).

80. See Yates, ibid., 2–3 and 6–7.

81. Ibid., 3.

82. Aristotle, *De memoria et reminiscentia*, 452a15 (Loeb edition; my translation).

83. Ibid.

84. Ibid., 452a25. Yates notes that the Scholastics used the first passages I cited to justify the artificial memory philosophically but states that she doubts Aristotle really had this distinction in mind. It is curious that she does not cite the passage I have just quoted on natural and customary memory, which would seem to confirm the Scholastic appeal. See Yates, *Art of Memory*, 35.

85. See Yates, ibid., 4–6.

86. *Ad C. Herrenium*, III.xvi.28–29 (Loeb edition; Bylan translation).

87. Cicero, *De inventione*, II.liii.160 (Loeb edition; Hubbel translation).

88. See Yates, *Art of Memory*, 20–21, 57.

89. See Lechner, *Renaissance Concepts*, 136, 150.

90. Ibid., 135.

91. Yates notes that Lullism departs completely from the classical tradition in its primarily logical and procedural bias. She points out that "what is totally absent from genuine Lullism as artificial memory is the use of images in the manner of the classical artificial memory of the rhetoric tradition. . . . It is more like a mystical and cosmological geometry and algebra" (*Art of Memory*, 185).

92. Charles Mosley, *A Century of Emblems* (Brookfield: Scholar's, 1992), 2.

93. Ibid., 7.

94. Ibid.

95. Ibid.

96. Ibid., 8.

97. Ibid.

98. See ibid., 10.

99. Ibid., 11.

100. See ibid., 15.

101. See ibid., 27. See also Yates, *Art of Memory*, 169.

102. Mosley, *Century of Emblems*, 28. For example, consider van der Noot's *A Theater wherein be representd as wel the miseries and calamities that follow the voluptuous Worldlings*, which was translated into many languages; or La Perrière's *Theater of Fine Devices*.

103. See ibid. Note Mosley's interesting discussion of how certain scenes in the plays of the time make sense only if one freezes certain moments into a tableau that is essentially an emblem; the emblem book and the theater merge.

104. Yates, *Art of Memory*, 169.

Chapter 6: The Discovery of the True Aristotle

1. Alessandro Giuliani, "Vico's Rhetorical Philosophy and the New Rhetoric," in *Giambattista Vico's Science of Humanity*, ed. Giorgio Tagliacozzo and Donald Phillip Verene (Baltimore: John Hopkins University Press, 1976), 31–46.

2. The distinction between primary and secondary rhetoric is George Kennedy's; it is pointed out in John D. Schaeffer, "From Wit to Narration: Vico's Theory of Metaphor in its Rhetorical Context," *New Vico Studies* 2 (1984): 59–73.

3. Giuliani, "Vico's Rhetorical Philosophy," 37.

4. See ibid., 38.

5. See Schaeffer, "From Wit to Narration," 59–61.

6. Dominique Bouhours, *La Manière da bien penser dans les ouvrages d'esprit* (1771), quoted by Schaeffer, "From Wit to Narration," 61.

7. Schaeffer, ibid., 61.

8. Baltasar Gracián, *Agudeza y arte de ingenio* (1649), Discurso II, quoted in Michael Mooney, *Vico in the Tradition of Rhetoric* (Princeton: Princeton University Press, 1985), 144.

9. Schaeffer, "From Wit to Narration," 60. Schaeffer gives as an example the image of the geometer's compass in John Donne's "Valediction: Forbidding Mourning." The conceit is, of course, that lovers' souls equal a compass. For a more general account of the conceitists, see Mooney, *Vico in the Tradition*, 142–149.

10. Gracián, *Agudeza*, Discurso II, quoted in Mooney, ibid., 144.

11. See Mooney, ibid., 145.

12. Schaeffer, "From Wit to Narration," 60.

13. Ibid., 61.

14. Joseph Mazzeo, quoted in Schaeffer, ibid., 61.

15. Schaeffer, ibid., 62.

16. Ibid.

17. A fact pointed out in Giuliani, "Vico's Rhetorical Philosophy," 35.

18. See ibid.

19. Ibid.

20. See ibid., 40.

21. See ibid.

22. Ibid., 41.

23. Ibid.

24. See ibid.

25. English translations of the *Institutiones oratoriae* are my own.

26. See Aristotle, *Poetics*, 22.6, and *Rhetoric*, 1412a.

27. Schaeffer, "From Wit to Narration," 64.

28. Giuliani, "Vico's Rhetorical Philosophy," 42.

29. Ibid.

30. Giambattista Vico, 'Oratio III,' in Vico, *Opere Filosofiche*, 739. This passage is pointed out by Giuliani, "Vico's Rhetorical Philosophy," 43.

31. See Giuliani, ibid., 42. Also see Mooney, *Vico in the Tradition*, 133–35.

32. See Mooney, ibid., 133.

33. William J. Grimaldi. *Studies in the Philosophy of Aristotle's* Rhetoric (Wiesbaden: Steiner, 1975), 55.

34. Ibid., 1. The classical locus of this critique, of course, is found in

Plato, particularly in the *Gorgias;* it is taken up by Descartes, Spinoza, Locke, and Kant, to name a few; and in the experience of any typical undergraduate (or graduate, for that matter) education in philosophy the critique is taken in, as it were, with the mother's milk. The commonplaces of this critique are too well known—and too tedious—to repeat (and are not the subject of this study). For an excellent analysis of the debate between philosophy and rhetoric (by a partisan of rhetoric) see Brian Vickers, *In Defence of Rhetoric* (Oxford: Clarendon, 1988). Also note Ernesto Grassi's *Rhetoric as Philosophy: The Humanistic Tradition* (University Park: Pennsylvania State University Press, 1980), referred to in Chapter 1.

35. Grimaldi, *Studies in Aristotle's* Rhetoric, 16.

36. All translations of Aristotle are my own.

37. Kennedy writes that "in Greek choral lyric, the metrical pattern of a *strophe,* or stanza, is repeated with different words in the *antistrophe*" (See *Aristotle: On Rhetoric,* trans. George A. Kennedy [New York: Oxford University Press, 1991], 28–29, fn. 2). He also notes that in using the word *antistrophē* Aristotle is consciously rejecting the analogy between the true and false arts in the *Gorgias.* There, you will recall, justice is called the *antistrophos* to medicine (464b8), and rhetoric, as a false form of justice, equals cookery, the false form of medicine (465c1–3). Since rhetoric, like dialectic, has no specific field of knowledge as its province but is a tool for use in all, Aristotle "avoids the fallacy of Plato's *Gorgias,* where Socrates is obsessed with finding some kind of knowledge specific to rhetoric" (ibid.).

38. See Grimaldi, *Studies in Aristotle's* Rhetoric, 56–57.

39. Ibid., 62.

40. Ibid. Grimaldi notes that the ancient commentator Minucianus says that the three *pisteis* are *ēthikai, pathētikai,* and *logikai ai autai kai pragmatikai;* and Dionysius of Halicarnassus refers to them as *pragma, pathos,* and *ēthos* (63; also note n. 11).

41. Ibid.

42. Ibid., 20–21.

43. Ibid., 136–137. And moreover, on this interpretation, the text of the *Rhetoric* becomes unified, and Aristotle is not needlessly convicted of gross contradiction and overly muddled thinking. For the philological details of this, see ibid., chaps. 1 and 2.

44. Ibid., 66.

45. See Aristotle, *Topics,* 162a15; also see Grimaldi, *Studies in Aristotle's* Rhetoric, 69.

46. Grimaldi, ibid., 69; also see *Topics,* 100a30.

47. See Terence Irwin's glossary to Aristotle, *Nicomachean Ethics,* trans. Terence Irwin (Indianapolis: Hackett, 1985), 397–98; also see Grimaldi, *Studies in Aristotle's* Rhetoric, 69.

48. See Grimaldi, ibid., 70.

49. Ibid.

50. Henry George Liddell and Robert Scott, *A Greek-English Lexicon*. Rev. and augmented Henry Stuart Jones (Oxford: Clarendon, 1968), entry under *thumos*.

51. Ibid. Grimaldi makes an interesting survey of the term and its cognates in some detail and shows convincingly the *logomorphism* involved in defining *en thumō* (*Studies in Aristotle's* Rhetoric, 71–80).

52. See Grimaldi, ibid., 82.

53. Ibid.

54. See ibid., 115.

55. Ibid., 126.

56. Ibid., 130.

57. Ibid., 131.

58. For a fuller discussion of the form of the enthymeme, see ibid., 87–88.

59. Ibid., 88.

60. Ibid., 136.

61. Theophrastus, quoted in ibid., 132.

62. Grimaldi, ibid., 133.

63. Liddell and Scott, *Greek-English Lexicon*, entry under *proairesis*.

64. See Irwin's glossary to Aristotle, *Nicomachean Ethics*, 392.

65. See Aristotle, *Nicomachean Ethics*, 1103a10ff., for example.

66. Liddell and Scott, *Greek-English Lexicon, proairesis*.

67. Also see Grimaldi, *Studies in Aristotle's* Rhetoric, 143.

68. See ibid., 141–44.

69. Neocles, quoted in Grimaldi, ibid., 150, in Greek; my translation. It is interesting to see that the "parts" of the enthymeme are referred to as "axioms."

70. Aeschines, quoted in Grimaldi, *Studies in Aristotle's* Rhetoric, 143.

Chapter 7: The Comic Nature of Geometric Method

1. See Edwin Arthur Burtt, *The Metaphysical Foundations of Modern Physical Science: A Historical and Critical Essay* (London: Routledge and Kegan Paul, 1950), 31.

2. René Descartes, quoted in L. J. Beck, *The Method of Descartes: A Study of the Regulae* (Oxford: Clarendon, 1952), 38.

3. Burtt, *Metaphysical Foundations*, 33.

4. Niccolò Tartaglia, quoted in Paul Lawrence Rose, *The Italian Renaissance of Mathematics: Studies on Humanists and Mathematicians from Petrarch to Galileo* (Geneva: Librairie Droz, 1975), 152.

5. See Rose, ibid., 151.

6. Ibid.

7. Ibid., 152.

8. Ibid., 156.

9. See ibid.

10. Ibid., 287.

11. Ibid.

12. See Burtt, *Metaphysical Foundations*, 31–32.

13. See ibid., 97.

14. Ibid., 97–98.

15. Beck, *Method of Descartes*, 44.

16. Ibid.

17. Ann Hartle, *Death and the Disinterested Spectator* (Albany: State University of New York Press, 1986), 182.

18. See ibid.

19. Ibid., 182.

20. Beck, *Method of Descartes*, 116.

21. Descartes, quoted in Beck, ibid., 120–22.

22. See Hartle, *Death and the Disinterested Spectator*, 182–84.

23. Eugenio Garin, "Vico and the Heritage of Renaissance Thought," in *Vico: Past and Present*, ed. Giorgio Tagliacozzo (Atlantic Highlands, N.J.: Humanities, 1981), 99–116.

24. See Elio Gianturco's note 2 to *SM*, 6–8.

25. Here I follow the views of Guido Fassò, "The Problem of Law and the Historical Origin of the *New Science*," in *Giambattista Vico's Science of Humanity*, ed. G. Tagliacozzo and D. P. Verene (Baltimore: Johns Hopkins University Press, 1976), 3–14, and Donald Phillip Verene, *The New Art of Autobiography: An Essay on the Life of Giambattista Vico Written by Himself* (Oxford: Clarendon, 1991), 137–147; I give these issues my own slant.

26. Giambattista Vico, *Opere Giurdiche*, ed. Paolo Cristofolini (Florence: Sansoni, 1974), 387.

27. Ibid.; my translation.

28. Verene, *New Art*, 146.

29. Verene, "Imaginative Universals and Narrative Truth," *New Vico Studies* 6 (1988): 12.

30. Donald Phillip Verene, *Vico's Science of the Imagination* (Ithaca, N.Y.: Cornell University Press, 1981), 113.

31. See ibid.

32. See ibid., 113–14.

33. For a general account of what Vico feigns, and of how we can understand it in relation to what Descartes feigns, see Donald Phillip Verene, *New Art*, 112–125. Here I concentrate on the optimism and imperative for reform of Cartesian method, as well as on the sense of the comic involved in the notion of an atemporal spectator.

34. René Descartes, *Philosophical Works of Descartes*, Vol. 1, trans. E. S. Haldane and G. R. T. Ross (New York: Dover, 1955), 83.

35. Verene, *New Art*, 115. Also see Hartle, 138.

36. Descartes, *Philosophical Works*, 89.

37. Ibid., 81. On Descartes's mock modesty and what he is feigning in his claims, see Hartle, *Death and the Disinterested Spectator*, 173–74.

38. Descartes, *Philosophical Works*, 83.

39. Ibid., 83–87.

40. Ibid., 99. See Hartle, *Death and the Disinterested Spectator*, 144.

41. Hartle, ibid., 145. It is interesting to note that Descartes likens the reading of ancient authors to travels in a foreign land, which have the same advantages and disadvantages; the ancients to him are comic as well. See Hartle, ibid., 139.

42. Ibid., 146.

43. Descartes, *Philosophical Works*, 154.

44. Ibid., 155.

45. On the "tether and tang of the particular," see C. S. Lewis, *Pilgrim's Regress* (Grand Rapids, Mich.: Eerdmans, 1933), 198.

46. Verene, *Vico's Science*, 114.

47. Verene, *New Art*, 86.

48. Ibid., 87. For a general account of autobiography in the life of the philosopher and its relation to his philosophy, see 208–231. Here I focus on the issue of reform and self-knowledge.

49. See Verene, "Philosophical Memory," *AA Files: Annals of the Architectural Association School of Architecture* 16 (Autumn 1987): 57–62.

50. Ibid.

51. See Attila Fáj, "Vico as a Philosopher of *Metabasis*," in Tagliacozzo and Verene, *Vico's Science of Humanity*, 87–109, and "The Unorthodox Logic of Scientific Discovery in Vico," in Tagliacozzo, *Vico: Past and Present*, 198–205. Fáj also considers *Ancient Wisdom* but offers no account of the development of Vico's views beyond his initial positions into the maturer vision of his new science. Fáj also makes no reference to Vico's work in jurisprudence, nor to Vico's account of his development in the *Autobiography*.

52. Fáj, "Unorthodox Logic," 198.

53. Ibid., 202.

54. Fáj, "Vico as Philosopher," 93.

55. Ibid., 108.

56. See ibid.

57. Fáj, "Unorthodox Logic," 205.

58. See Leon Pompa, *Vico: A Study of the* New Science. 2d ed. (Cambridge: Cambridge University Press, 1990).

59. See ibid., "Appendix: Humanist Interpretation."

60. Max Fisch, "Comment on Professor Pompa's Paper," in *Vico and Contemporary Thought*, ed. G. Tagliacozzo, M. Mooney, and D. P. Verene (Atlantic Highlands, N.J.: Humanities , 1976), 56. Thanks to Randall E. Auxier for pointing out this passage to me.

61. Pompa, *Study*, 186.

Chapter 8: What Is Worth Thinking?

1. Bruno Migliorini, *The Italian Language*, trans. T. Gwyfnor Griffith (London: Faber and Faber, 1966), 306.

2. Ibid, 306. Also see Mario Fubini, *Stile e umanità di Giambattista Vico*, 2d ed. (Milan: Riccordo Ricciardi, 1965); especially note "La Lingua del Vico," 83–134. On the rhetorical notion of purity of language, see Friedrich Nietzsche, *Friedrich Nietzsche on Rhetoric and Language: With the Full Text of His Lectures on Rhetoric*, ed. and trans. Sandra L. Gilman, Carole Blair, and Daniel J. Parent (Oxford: Oxford University Press, 1989), 29.

3. Migliorini, *Italian Language*, 334.

4. Ibid., 335.

5. Salvatore Battaglia, *Grande dizionario della lingue Italiana*, Vol. IV (Turin: Unione Tipografico, 1966), entry under *degnità*.

6. Armand L. De Gaetano, *Giambattista Gelli and the Florentine Academy: The Rebellion against Latin* (Florence: Leo S. Olschiki, 1976), 42–43.

7. Ibid., 43.

8. Ibid. Gelli's belief in the *giganti* is suggestive, given Vico's statements on them as well.

9. See ibid.

10. See Nicolini, *Commento storico alla seconda Scienza Nuova*, Vols. 1 and 2 (Rome: Edizioni di Storia e Letteratura, 1978), Vol. 1, 107, n. 305.

11. See De Gaetano's account, *Gelli and the Florentine Academy*, 100–132.

12. Ibid., 155.

13. Charlton T. Lewis and Charles Short, *A Latin Dictionary* (Oxford: Clarendon Press, 1980), entry under *axioma*.

14. Henry George Liddell and Robert Scott, *A Greek-English Lexicon*. Rev. and augmented Henry Stuart Jones (Oxford: Clarendon), 1968, entry under *axioō*.

15. Ibid.

16. Ibid., entry under *axioma*.

17. Ibid.

18. Ibid.

19. *The Cambridge Italian Dictionary*, ed. Barbara Reynolds (Cambridge: Cambridge University Press, 1981), Vol. 1, entry under *degnare*.

20. Ibid., entry under *degnità*.

21. *Grande dizionario*, entry under *degnità*, my translation.

22. *Cambridge Italian Dictionary*, entry under *assioma*.

23. See Nietzsche, 29. There he states that "by *proprietas*, in the rhetorical sense, one understands that expression which most completely signifies an object." The term *assioma* lacks *proprietas* in terms of Vico's new science.

24. Donald Phillip Verene, *The New Art of Autobiography: An Essay on the Life of Giambattista Vico Written by Himself* (Oxford: Clarendon, 1991), 21.

25. Ibid., 21–22.

26. H. P. Adams, *The Life and Works of Giambattista Vico* (London: Allen and Unwin, 1935), 173.

27. Ibid.

28. See, for example, Vico's letter to Francesco Saverio Estevan (January 12, 1729), in *Vico: Opere*, ed. Fausto Nicolini (Milan: Riccordo Ricciardi, 1953), 139.

29. Fubini, *Stile e umanità*, 20–21.

30. Fausto Nicolini, quoted in Fubini, ibid., 21, n. 1.

31. Christopher Maurer, "Translator's Introduction." In Baltasar Gracián, *The Art of Worldly Wisdom*, trans. Christopher Maurer (New York: Doubleday, 1992), xv.

32. Adams, *Life and Works*, 185.

33. G. F. Finetti, quoted in Verene, *New Art*, 31.

34. Gregory Vlastos, *Socrates: Ironist and Moral Philosopher* (Cambridge: Cambridge University Press, 1991), 31.

35. Donald Phillip Verene, introduction to *On Humanistic Education: Six Inaugural Orations, 1699–1707,* trans. G. A. Pinton and A. W. Shipee. (Ithaca, N.Y.: Cornell University Press, 1993), 2.

36. Liddell and Scott, *Greek-English Lexicon,* entry under sēma.

37. Ibid. My particular thanks to Nancy du Bois for pointing this out to me. My conversations with her on this subject helped greatly in developing this section.

38. Giuseppe Mazzotta, "Vico's Encyclopedia," *Yale Journal of Criticism* 1:2 (Spring 1988): 65–79.

39. Ibid., 68.

40. Ibid., 76.

41. Ibid.

42. Ibid.

43. Ibid., 69.

44. Ibid.

45. Ibid.

46. Johann Georg Hamann, letter to F. H. Jacobi (January 18, 1776), in *Johann Georg Hamann's, des Magus im Norden, Leben und Schriften.* Vol. 4, *Hamann's Briefwechsel mit Friedrich Heinrich Jacobi.* Ed. C. H. Gildmeister (Gotha: Friedrich Andreas Perthes, 1868).

47. Donald Phillip Verene, "Philosophical Memory," *AA Files: Annals of the Architectural Association School of Architecture* 16 (Autumn 1987): 57–62.

48. Mazzotta, "Vico's Encyclopedia," 67.

49. Aristotle, *Poetics* IX.2–3 (Loeb edition; my translation).

50. Ibid., IX.3–4; my translation.

51. Verene, "Philosophical Memory," 61.

52. Ibid., 58.

53. Ibid.

54. Here I follow Verene's lead in "Philosophical Memory."

55. Frances Yates, *The Art of Memory* (Chicago: Chicago University Press, 1966), 169.

56. Ibid., 129.

57. Wenneker Lu Beery, "An Examination of 'L'Idea del Theatro' of Giulio Camillo, including an Annotated Translation, with Special Attention to His Influence on Emblem Literature and Iconography" (Ph.D. diss., University of Pittsburgh, 1970), 17.

58. No modern critical edition of this work exists. A copy of Giulio Camillo, *L'Idea del theatro dell'eccelen. M. Giulio Camillo*, ed. Lodovico Domeniche (Florence: Apresso Lorenzo Torrentino, 1550), can be found in the Biblioteca Nazionale in Florence. A photocopy of this can be found in the Vico Institute, Emory University, Atlanta, Georgia. Also see Lina Bolzoni, *Il Teatro della memoria: Studi su Giulio Camillo* (Padua: Liviana Editrice, 1984).

59. Marco Frascari, *Monsters of Architecture: Anthropomorphism in Architectural Theory* (Savage: Bowman, 1991), 25.

60. Erasmus, *Epistolae*, 10, 29–30, quoted in Yates, *Art of Memory*, 132.

61. Ibid.

62. Beery, "Examination of 'L'Idea del Theatro,'" 11.

63. Yates, *Art of Memory*, 137. For a complete description of this fantastic *fabbrica*, see chap. 6. For a further understanding of its function in terms of architectural memory and bodily imagery, see Frascari, *Monsters of Architecture*, 21–25.

64. Frascari, ibid., 25.

65. Giulio Camillo Delmino, quoted in Beery, "Examination of 'L'Idea del Theatro,'" 58.

66. Beery, ibid.

67. Frascari, *Monsters of Architecture*, 25.

68. Giulio Camillo Delmino, *L'Idea del theatro*, quoted in Yates, *Art of Memory*, 138.

69. Ibid.

70. Verene, "Philosophical Memory," 61.

71. Ibid., 17.

72. See Frascari, *Monsters of Architecture*, 26.

73. Yates, *Art of Memory*, 145.

74. This may sound like an exaggeration, but it is not. See ibid., 129–130.

75. I here disagree here with Verene, who states that the *Scienza nuova* is *solely* a theater of words; the idea of the emblem book complicates the issue a little.

76. Also see Verene, "Philosophical Memory," 62.

77. Ibid., 22.

78. There is an excellent description of the frontispiece in Donald Phillip Verene, *Vico's Science of the Imagination* (Ithaca, N. Y.: Cornell University Press, 1981), 1: "God appears in the sky as an eye within a triangle, reflecting his vision onto the breast of a female figure of metaphysic who surmounts a globe representing the world of nature. In addition to this abstract symbol of nature we see thick clouds and forest surrounding a clearing in which are spread out various objects of the world of civil society, prominent among which is a fasces representing the origin of civil law. To the left, illuminated by a ray reflected from the breast of metaphysic, is a statue of Homer, the first known poet of Western tradition. In the middle, separating the earth from the sky and the forest from the clearing, and by one of its corners supporting metaphysic and the globe of nature, is a stone altar, upon which, among other objects, is placed a lituus for taking auguries, signifying divination. The picture distinguishes the divine from the world and, within the world, the natural from the human. In the framework of these two separations appear the oppositions of darkness and light, earth and sky, forest and clearing, divination and civil practice, metaphysics and poetry."

79. Donald Phillip Verene, "The New Art of Narration: Vico and the Muses," *New Vico Studies* 1 (1983): 21–38.

80. See Yates, *Art of Memory*, 136.

81. Verene, "Philosophical Memory," 62.

82. William J. Grimaldi, *Studies in the Philosophy of Aristotle's Rhetoric* (Wiesbaden: Steiner, 1975), 126.

83. Theophrastus, quoted in Grimaldi, ibid., 132.

84. Aeschines, quoted in Grimaldi, ibid., 143.

85. Liddell and Scott, *Greek-English Lexicon*, entry under *proairesis*.

Chapter 9: Conclusion

1. Compare this axiom with Cicero's statement that "the order of the places will preserve the order of things, and the images of things will denote the things themselves." *De oratoria*, II.lxxxvi.352–353 (Loeb edition; translation follows the more literal reading offered by Frances Yates, *The Art of Memory* [Chicago: Chicago University Press, 1966], 2).

2. Giorgio Tagliacozzo, epilogue to *Giambattista Vico: An International Symposium*, ed. Giorgio Tagliacozzo and Hayden V. White (Baltimore: Johns Hopkins University Press, 1969), 599–600, n. 3. Also see Donald Phillip Verene, *Vico's Science of the Imagination* (Ithaca, N. Y.: Cornell University Press, 1981), 207–208. Verene first drew my attention to the implications of the image of the tree of knowledge for understanding Vico's notion of sapienza poetica. I find myself in basic agreement with the account he offers in chapter 7 of *Vico's Science:* his analysis underlies mine. Also see Verene, "A Note on Vico's Tree of Knowledge." Paper presented at the meeting of the "Istituto Italiano di Cultura," Toronto, Octo-

ber 25, 1991. The commentator who has done the most with the image of the tree in relation to Vico is Mario Papini, *Arbor humanae linguae* (Bologna: Cappelli, 1984).

3. Frances Yates, *Art of Memory*, 186–187; note esp. figure 7 on page 186. Of course, as Verene notes, the image of a tree of knowledge is a very ancient one indeed, going back to the tree in Genesis 2:9 and found as the *axis mundi* connecting the three levels of the cosmos in archaic thought. See Verene, *Vico's Science*, 1–3.

4. Yates, *Art of Memory*, 187.

5. Ibid., 248.

6. See Tagliacozzo's epilogue, 600, n. 3.

7. Frances Bacon, *De dignatate et augmentis scientiarum*, in Bacon, *Essays, Advancement of Learning, New Atlantis, and Other Pieces*, ed. Richard Foster Jones (New York: Odyssey, 1937), 406.

8. Ibid.

9. Ibid.

10. Verene, *Vico's Science*, 208.

11. René Descartes, *Philosophical Works of Descartes*, Vol. 1, trans. E. S. Haldane and G. R. T. Ross (New York: Dover, 1955), 211.

12. See Verene, *Vico's Science*, 209. Verene notes that though Descartes speaks here of moral wisdom, he never really investigated nor developed the concept in his works.

13. Ibid.

14. See ibid.

15. Ibid., 209.

16. Ernst Cassirer, *Philosophy of Symbolic Forms*, Vol. 1 (New Haven: Yale University Press, 1955), 180. The Cassirer connection is discussed in Verene, *Vico's Science*, 210.

17. W. Wundt, quoted in Cassirer, *Philosophy*, 180–181.

18. Ibid., 181.

19. See Cassirer, ibid.

20. Ibid., 181–182.

21. See ibid., 183.

22. Ibid.

23. Ibid., 183–84.

24. Ibid., 319.

25. Verene, *Vico's Science*, 210.

26. See ibid., 210–211.

27. See ibid.

28. Ibid., 211.

29. See G. W. F. Hegel, *Phenomenology of Spirit*, trans. A. V. Miller (Oxford: Oxford University Press, 1981), para. 7. I am here, of course, only borrowing Hegel's *images*, which are to my mind the true essence of his genius. Any resemblance between his actual doctrine and mine is purely coincidental (and the names have been changed to protect the innocent).

30. Ibid., para. 8.

31. See ibid., paras. 10 and 15.

Index

Achilles, 27

Adams, H. P., 112, 114

Ad Herrenium, 65

Aeschines, 86, 128

Anabasis (*anabainō*): as heroic journey, xii, 2; as *katabasis*, 1; meaning of, 1; of Vico, 3, 124, 139

Apel, Karl-Otto, 6

Apthonius, 54

Aquinas, Thomas, 65

Arbor scientiae: Vico's vs. Bacon's, 119; of Lull, 131; theme of, 131; of Vico, 131–138; of Bacon, 132; of Bruno, 132; of Descartes, 132; Vico's vs. Descartes's, 132–133

Archimedes, 90

Aristotle, xiii, 53, 69, 71, 74, 114, 128, 129, 135; and origin of topical method, 54; on commonplace books, 63; on artificial memory, 64, 65; Vico's account of, 77; on enthymeme, 78–87; on rhetorical syllogism, 82; on antithesis, 83; on enthymemic knowledge, 83; on maxim (*gnomē*), 85–87; on poetry and history, 120

Augustine, Saint, 60

Averroës, 51

Axiom(s): as key to Vico's system, xii, 106; in Greek and Latin, 110; and deductive madness, 126

—of Vico: and deductive model, xii; circulation of, through book of wisdom, xiv, 108, 116, 124; concerned with the true and the certain, 95; refutative, 95; as "thoughts worth thinking," 108, 110; as *assioma*, 111; as gnomic enthymeme, 115, 116, 128–129, 130; and chronological table of *New Science*, 124–125; in *New Science*, 124–129; and frontispiece of *New Science*, 125; as alphabet of culture, 126; and origins, 126; and providence, 126, 127; and Camillo's Theater of Memory, 127; and eloquence, 127; and history, 127; as *pisteis*, 127; and archaic logic, 128; general and particular, 128; as master images, 128; and imagination, 129; and microcosm, 130; mimetic and indicative, 136; temporal dimension, 137. See also *Degnità*

Bacon, Francis, 113, 119, 120; style of, 62; and commonplace books, 63; and tree of knowledge, 132

Barfield, Owen, xii, xiii, 27–39 *passim*

Baroque conceit: debate over, 70–71; Cartesian critique of, 71; as *entimemo urbano*, 71; combines beauty and truth, 74; as enthymemic, 74–75

167

phor of wax, 102–103; tree of knowledge of, 132. *See also* Cartesian (Cartesianism)

Diacetto, Francesco da, 9

Diogenes Laertius, 56

Divination, 97, 98–99, 117

Divine: in history, 15; distinguished from human, 16; interacting with human, 19

Doria, Paolo Mattia, 49

Elocution: primary in Vico, 72

Eloquence, 3, 21, 51, 130; in Renaissance, 10–12; despised by Cartesians, 15; and prudence, 59; and morality, 62; and logic, 74; and irony, 115; and clarity, 125; and *degnità*, 125, 127

Emblem book(s): as memory systems, 65–68; imagination in, 66; and *ingenium*, 66; and morality, 66; nonliteral signification in, 66; and metaphor, 66–67; and maxims, 67; methodology of, 67; as *theatrum mundi*, 68; and topical method, 68; *Scienza nuova* as, 123–124

Enthymeme: and Demosthenes, 51; combines reason and emotion, 79, 87; misunderstandings about, 79–81; as body of persuasion, 80; combines *ēthos*, *pathos*, and *logos*, 80; central to rhetoric, 80–81; correlative to syllogism, 81; prior to Aristotle, 81–82; and topics, 82; not abbreviated syllogism, 83, 105; not analytic, 87; as gnomic, 114; and axiomatic method, 139

Epicureans, 18, 46, 97

Epicurus, 46

Erasmus, 121

Euclid: method of, 2, 3; prestige of, 88, 90

Fable (*fabula, favola*), 23, 129; as making human world, 26; as truth, 26, 32; ignored, 43; enthymemic, 135

Fáj, Attila, 104–106, 107

Fantasia. See Maker's imagination

Fassò, Guido, 95

Ficino, Marsilio, 5, 9, 14, 17, 67

Finetti, G. F., 115

Fisch, Max, 1, 44, 107, 108

Flamino, Marc Antonio, 122

Florentine Academy, 110, 111

Frascari, Marco, 121, 122

Fubini, Mario, 113

Galileo, 11, 12, 14, 17, 88, 90, 114

Garin, Eugenio, 92

Gelli, Giambattista Domenico, 109–110

Geometrical method: errors of, 13; of Vico, 47; Cartesian, 51; quest for, 90–91; comic nature of, 100; and detachment, 102; and history, 102; and memory, 102

Geometry: as model for life, 3; as made by humans, 16; as quest for certainty, 90–91; rejects memory, 91–92; as analysis, 93; misapplied to physics, 93; of Vico's new science, 127; of melancholy, 138–139

Giuliani, Alessandro, 69–77 *passim*

Giumballari, Pier Francesco, 110

God: imitation of, 9–10, 15, 16, 19, 20, 34, 47, 99; as maker, 16, 19

origins, 37; as self-knowledge, 52; satisfies intellect, 96

Making: divine and human, 20

Mathematics: Renaissance revival of, xii, 88; as human creation, 9, 17, 34; different from physics, 17; errors of, 17; and "minute wits," 21

Maurer, Christopher, 62, 113

Maxim (*gnomē*): in Vico, 73–74; combines beauty and truth, 74; enthymemic, 74, 76, 86; not abbreviated syllogism, 78; as *proairesis*, 85; as ethical, 85–86; in Aristotle, 85–87; and moral choice, 129; as sensory topic, 129

Mazzotta, Giuseppe, 118, 119

Melancholy, xiv, 47; geometry of, 138–139

Memory (MEMORIA): logic of, 2; and algebra, 13; as method, 21; as return to origins, 21; science of, 21; as imagination, 21, 22, 43; and archaic consciousness, 38; three aspects of, 39–42; in *New Science*, 40–42; and self-awareness, 43; as historical, 45; and rhetoric, 57; artificial, 63, 65; as place of images, 64; natural vs. artificial, 65; and death's pageants, 118; theater of, 119–123; systems of Renaissance, 120

Metaphor: as creating experience, 32; and identity, 32; as basis for epistemology and logic, 33

Metaphysics: proof of, 22, 23; task of, 24; bodily, 30–31, 123, 133; imaginative, 34; and human frailty, 34, 94, 122; as poetic, 38; principles

of, 39; of the concept, 46; and words, 117, 119; starting place of, 118; and myth, 120; and images, 122–123; and providence, 125

Method: of Vico's anabasis, 2–4; of modernity, 17–18

Microcosm, 7–9, 12, 13, 17, 20, 30, 34, 51, 68, 103, 120, 122, 130; false image of, 14; of *Scienza nuova*, 124

Migliorini, Bruno, 108, 109

Mooney, Michael, 6–7, 77

Mosley, Charles, 66, 67, 123

Neocles, 86

Neptune, 31

New sciences, 88, 92, 100. *See also* Vico, Giambattista: new science of

Nicholas of Cusa, 5, 7, 8, 9

Nicolini, Fausto, 113

Norlin, George, 58

Odysseus, 27

Orcus, 23; as chaos, 24

Pan, 23

Paracelsus, 8

Peregrini, M., 74

Perrault, Charles, 49

Philology, 15; defined, 21; deals with certains, 45; and certainty, 95; converted to philosophy, 97

Philosophy: history of, xii–xiii; usefulness of, 18; examines philology, 21, 95, 97, 117, 120, 128; and truth, 95; of history, 118

Physics: as certain, 16; of first humans, 23; as speculative, 94

84–85; sensory, 119, 129; and *degnità* (axioms), 126, 128
Tree of knowledge. See *Arbor scientiae*
True (*il vero, vera; verum*), 20; as made, 16, 19, 29, 33, 34; as convertible with made, 17, 19
Tuscanism, 108–109

Untersteiner, Mario, 56

Verba and *res*, 56–57, 66, 73, 76, 121, 128
Verene, Donald Phillip, 5, 24, 29, 33, 35, 39, 42, 46, 52, 96, 100, 103, 106, 116, 119, 123, 127, 132, 135, 136
Vico, Giambattista: and rhetoric, xi, 4, 6–7, 12, 49; coherence of, xi–xii, 48; as guide, 3; and Renaissance, 4; development of, 5; as humanist, 6–7; as metaphysician, 15; and historicism, 18; descent of, 50; Aristotelianism of, 77; and geometric method, 92–94; unorthodox science of, 106; irony of, 107, 115–116; and Tuscanism, 109; and geometric nomenclature, 114, 115, 116; as philosopher, 115
—new science of: coherence of, xi–xii, xiii; master key of, 22; as learned ignorance, 35, 37, 41, 98, 99, 100, 124; method of, 43; and other new sciences, 93–94; as a new critical art, 95; as rational civil theology, 97–100; as divination, 98–99; demonstrates providence, 98–100; task in third age, 104; vocabulary of, 123–124
—*Scienza nuova* (*New Science*), xi, xiv, 1, 2, 3, 5, 7, 17, 22, 29, 34, 37, 38, 40, 42, 43, 44, 49, 94, 106, 108, 113, 114, 115, 118, 120, 128, 129, 130, 131, 136; as book of wisdom, xiv, 107; as memory system, 68; and self-knowledge, 107; in negative and positive form, 111; editions of, 111, 112–113; style of, 112–116; style and terminology of, 114; as memory system, 121; as emblem book, 123–129; as theater of memory, 123–129; argument in, 126; and reader of, 127; as rhetorical speech, 127; method of, 139
—Other works: *Ancient Wisdom*, 16, 34, 41, 74, 106; *Autobiography*, 4, 13, 16, 21, 40, 42, 95, 100, 106; *De constantia jurisprudentis*, 95; *Disputation*, 72; *Institutes of Oratory*, 49, 72, 73, 74, 104, 128; *Study Methods*, 13, 39, 40, 49, 50, 72, 104, 106; *Universal Law*, 113
Vlastos, Gregory, 115

Wisdom (*sapientia*), 130, 132; and the whole, 20; as learned ignorance, 37; requires enthymeme, 87; human and divine, 97, 136; as self-knowledge, 100; concerns intellect and will, 131; as poetic, 131; as melancholy, 138–139
Witnessing consciousness (*coscienza*), 3, 15–17, 19–20, 39, 43, 94, 96, 100, 131, 133, 136

Yates, Frances, 57, 64, 65, 120, 123, 131

Zeno, 61